OFFICIALS & STAFF

BOARD OF DIRECTORS

INDIANAPOLIS MOTOR SPEEDWAY CORPORATION

Mary Fendrich Hulman
Chairman of the Board Emeritus

Mari Hulman George
Chairman of the Board

Anton Hulman George   **M. Josephine George**

Katherine M. George   **Nancy L. George**   **Jack R. Snyder**

OFFICERS

Jeffrey G. Belskus
Executive Vice President & Treasurer

William R. Donaldson
Vice President

Anton Hulman George
President & CEO

Jack R. Snyder
Assistant Secretary

Peggy Swalls
Secretary

ADDITIONAL STAFF

Don Bailey

Brian Barnhart
Superintendent

Dr. Henry Bock
Director, Medical Services

W. Curtis Brighton
Vice President

Lee Driggers
Computer Resources

Kevin Forbes
Director, Engineering & Design

Mel Harder
Property Manager

Pat Hayes
Controller

Kurt Hunt
Marketing Coordinator

Ron King
Food & Beverage Manager

Ralph Kramer
Director, Hall of Fame Museum

Kent Liffick
Director, Special Events

Bruce Lynch
Retail Merchandising Manager

Robert McInteer
Director, Safety

Ron McQueeney
Director, Photography

Gloria Novotney
Director, Credentials

Bob Walters
Director, Public Relations

INDY RACING LEAGUE

Jack Long
Executive Director

Tom Binford
Commissioner

**Robin Burger, Phil Casey, Joie Chitwood, Tiffany Hemmer,
Cindy Napier, Johnny Rutherford, Jan Shaffer**
Indy Racing League Staff

CONTENTS

PAGE 8

PAGE 18

PAGE 54

Published by:
Indy Publications, IMS Corporation.
Director:
William R. Donaldson
Executive Editor:
Kurt D. Hunt
Editor:
Dawn M. Bair
Graphic Design:
Frederick Jungclaus & Michael Kreffel
Editorial Contributions:
Jan Shaffer, Bruce Martin, Mark Robinson,
Donald Davidson and Beth Walkup.

INDY PUBLICATIONS
INDY REVIEW VOLUME 6, 1996
ISBN 1-880526-05-0
Library of Congress ISSN 1059-3179

Thank You 4
IRL Co-Champions 6
A Memorable Event 8
The Desert Heat 18
Indianapolis 500 Entry List 24
Trackside Files 26
500 Festival 50
Before the Roar 52
The Commitment To Run 54
Month of Speed 62
The 33 Starters 66
For Those Who Tried 100
Epilogue 104
IRL Awards 106
Indy 200 at Walt Disney World Awards 107
Dura-Lube 200 Awards 108
Indy 500 Contingency Awards 109
Indy 500 Special Incentive Awards 110
USAC and Officials 112
IRL Final Point Standings 113
Indy 200 at Walt Disney World Starting Lineup 114
Indy 200 at Walt Disney World Official Box Score 115
Dura-Lube 200 Starting Lineup 116
Dura-Lube 200 Official Box Score 117
Daily Practice Laps 118
Daily Practice Speeds 120
Qualification Attempt Summary 122
Starting Lineup 123
Interval Scoring 124
Official Box Score 125
Indy's Career Top Ten 126
Photo Credits 127
Marks of Tradition 128

3

When Buddy Lazier took the checkered flag to win the 80th Indianapolis 500, it served to underscore the magic of this great event. Driving a superb race in a car expertly prepared by the Ron Hemelgarn racing team, Buddy raced his way to the front in a contest as thrilling as any we have ever witnessed. It was a challenging month with a memorable outcome.

All of us at the Speedway congratulate Buddy, Ron, the crew and sponsors on their accomplishment, and invite you to share the dramatic events of this past May in Indianapolis. We are also proud to include a review of the 1996 races at Walt Disney World and Phoenix which marked the beginning of Indy Racing League competition. Those events, along with Indy, give us our first IRL driver champions - Buzz Calkins and Scott Sharp; and our first entrant champion - AJ Foyt Enterprises.

The following pages of our fifth *Indy Review* go out with my warmest congratulations to the champions, and my thanks to the racing fans and competitors.

Sincerely,

Tony George
President

Indianapolis
Motor
Speedway

Scott
Sharp

Buzz
Calkins

6

Indy 200

AT WALT DISNEY WORLD
INAUGURAL RACE • JANUARY 27, 1996

EVENT
REVIEW

INDY RACING LEAGUE

Indy 200
AT WALT DISNEY WORLD
INAUGURAL RACE · JANUARY 27, 1996

A Memorable

By Bruce Martin

Throughout its history, the Indianapolis 500 has represented the pinnacle of racing achievement for race drivers throughout the world who have dreamed of competing at the 2.5-mile Indianapolis Motor Speedway. But the path to the world's most famous race course has often been detoured with obstacles.

Over the past 17 years, there was no clear cut way for grass roots race drivers to compete in the Indianapolis 500. One path was through the Championship Auto Racing Teams (CART) series, but as that organization began to move away from oval track racing to a schedule dominated with street and road courses, the opportunity for oval track racers began to diminish. An emphasis was placed on drivers with road racing backgrounds, which meant drivers from open wheel, oval track racing were at a disadvantage.

That led Indianapolis Motor Speedway president Tony George to create the Indy Racing League, which features the Indianapolis 500 as its centerpiece event. The path to the Indianapolis 500 now runs through the IRL and its first stop for the 1996

Mickey Mouse rode along with Indy 200 winner Buzz Calkins for the victory lap.

season began at Disney World near the entrance to the Magic Kingdom on Jan. 27. And by the end of the Indy 200, the new league had created several new racing stars and enjoyed a magical beginning.

As teams arrived at Walt Disney World Speedway to prepare for the inaugural race of the Indy Racing League, George's vision was about to become a reality. The 1.0-mile oval located near the entrance to the Magic Kingdom was ready to stage a memorable event.

More importantly, this first IRL race was

the doorway for these drivers to the Indianapolis 500.

"For any race car driver in the world, no matter where you are, competing in the Indianapolis 500 is a dream," said Richie Hearn, the 1995 Formula Atlantic champion. "The first step to the Indianapolis 500 will come in the Indy 200 at Walt Disney World."

While Hearn represented road course racing, Tony Stewart was the pride of the United States Auto Club (USAC). The 24-year-old driver from Rushville, Ind. was the first driver in

9

Indy 200 AT WALT DISNEY WORLD
INAUGURAL RACE • JANUARY 27, 1996

**Above:
Opening ceremonies were car-
ried out in Disney's usual spectacular fanfare fashion.
Right: Drivers prepared to launch the inaugural Indy
Racing League season.**

auto racing history to win three national driving titles in the same season when he won
the USAC Midget, Sprint and Silver Crown
titles in 1995. In January, Stewart joined Team
Menard, which also included 1995
Indianapolis 500 pole winner Scott Brayton
and Eddie Cheever.

"I have to go through the learning curve all
over again," Stewart said. "In midgets and
sprint cars, you have the motor in front of

you and when you go to a rear-engine car, it
is a big change."

While drivers such as Hearn and Stewart
represent the future, Arie Luyendyk has
achieved success in the past with his victory
in the 1990 Indianapolis 500. He hopes to continue that success in the IRL.

"It is a no-brainer to realize the track at
Disney is in a good location, near the
entrance to the Magic Kingdom," Luyendyk

said. "I thought they did a really good job on the track. The surface and the layout is outstanding. But it is going to be a little bit difficult because it is such a fast track."

Hearn proved that in the first practice session when he turned a lap at 181.827 miles an hour. Buzz Calkins was the fourth fastest of the session behind Hearn, Buddy Lazier and Roberto Guerrero. The Indy Lights driver showed that he should not be overlooked.

"This is a new experience for me because it is my first Indy car race," Calkins said. "It is challenging. There are the usual butterflies that go with being in your first Indy car race, but there are a number of other drivers in the same position I'm in being their first race."

Lazier visited Disneyland as a child, but his first trip to Walt Disney World was more fun. Lazier captured the pole for the Indy 200 with a lap of 181.388 miles an hour on Jan. 26.

"Without question, this is the best ride at Disney World there is," said the 28-year-old Lazier. "It was a big moment to qualify for the Indianapolis 500 for the first time in 1991, but this ranks right up there with that accom-

Leading
the first 28 laps of the
first Indy 200 at Walt Disney World was
pole winner Buddy Lazier. Scott Sharp (above) finished
the day in 11th place after tangling with Eddie Cheever in the first turn.

plishment.

"It feels extremely good to win the pole. From the testing we have done, we are going to be all right in this series. We are doing the right things and it is paying off."

A crowd of over 35,000 fans witnessed the pole qualifications at the oval with a sellout crowd of 51,000 fans awaiting the race.

"Look at the stands," said Ron Hemelgarn, Lazier's team owner "This is real. This is not going to go away.

"These aren't second-class guys in this series. I'm proud to be a part of the IRL."

Hearn was the second fastest in qualifications, with a lap at 180.905 mph. But the young Californian driver crashed in the final practice session when he collided with Cheever in the first turn. His team was loaned a car by Pagan Racing and Hearn started 19th in the field.

Eliseo Salazar had the only serious crash at Orlando when he destroyed his Scandia Lola/

Ford-Cosworth in the first turn wall during Friday's practice. Salazar suffered a broken right leg which would force him to miss the next race at Phoenix.

As race day dawned with a great deal of anticipation for the beginning of the new league, Calkins and Stewart gave the newest racing series in the world two of its newest stars. In a battle of 24 year olds, Calkins was able to hold off Stewart to win the Indy 200.

After winning the race, Calkins posed with Mickey Mouse in victory lane and said, "Now that I've won the Indy 200 at Walt Disney World, I'm going to Indy!"

Calkins led the race twice for 130 laps and defeated Stewart by .866 seconds in a surprisingly competitive race. And most of the goals of the IRL were achieved during its glorious debut in front of 51,000 sun-splashed spectators at Walt Disney World and a national television audience on ABC.

This race showcased drivers capable of

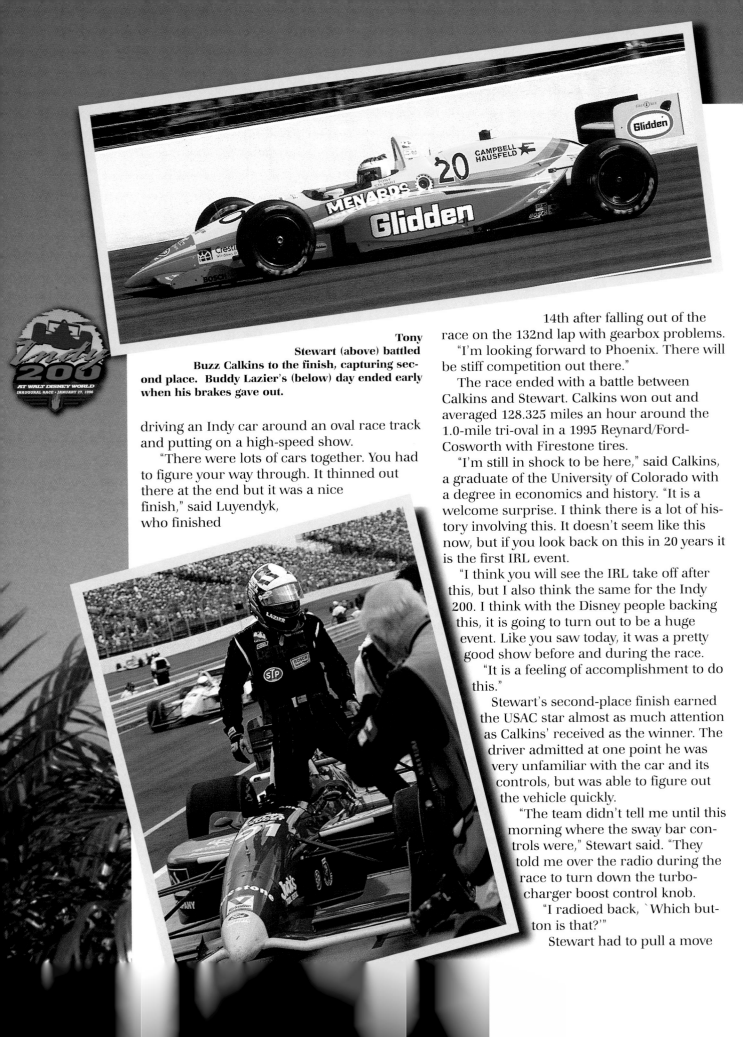

Tony Stewart (above) battled Buzz Calkins to the finish, capturing second place. Buddy Lazier's (below) day ended early when his brakes gave out.

driving an Indy car around an oval race track and putting on a high-speed show.

"There were lots of cars together. You had to figure your way through. It thinned out there at the end but it was a nice finish," said Luyendyk, who finished 14th after falling out of the race on the 132nd lap with gearbox problems.

"I'm looking forward to Phoenix. There will be stiff competition out there."

The race ended with a battle between Calkins and Stewart. Calkins won out and averaged 128.325 miles an hour around the 1.0-mile tri-oval in a 1995 Reynard/Ford-Cosworth with Firestone tires.

"I'm still in shock to be here," said Calkins, a graduate of the University of Colorado with a degree in economics and history. "It is a welcome surprise. I think there is a lot of history involving this. It doesn't seem like this now, but if you look back on this in 20 years it is the first IRL event.

"I think you will see the IRL take off after this, but I also think the same for the Indy 200. I think with the Disney people backing this, it is going to turn out to be a huge event. Like you saw today, it was a pretty good show before and during the race.

"It is a feeling of accomplishment to do this."

Stewart's second-place finish earned the USAC star almost as much attention as Calkins' received as the winner. The driver admitted at one point he was very unfamiliar with the car and its controls, but was able to figure out the vehicle quickly.

"The team didn't tell me until this morning where the sway bar controls were," Stewart said. "They told me over the radio during the race to turn down the turbo-charger boost control knob.

"I radioed back, `Which button is that?'"

Stewart had to pull a move

that would have made a veteran proud late in the race when he avoided a safety vehicle that was on the course tending to a crash. It started when Cheever drove down on Scott Sharp in the first turn sending both cars into the wall.

That set up one of the most bizarre scenes since Dennis Vitolo landed on Nigel Mansell's car in the pit entrance lane in the 1994 Indianapolis 500. Stewart was cut off by a safety vehicle and had to weave through the site of the wreckage like it was a ski slalom. His right-side wheels smacked the wall and he drove over debris, which could have possibly cut his tires.

"I was surprised I didn't get taken out of the race there," Stewart said. "It really surprised me. I hit it pretty hard. I just tried to hit the wheel flat against the wall. I ran over a lot of debris. We are real lucky we didn't puncture a tire or hurt the suspension."

When the race was restarted with five laps to go, Calkins was able to increase his lead to claim the historic victory.

"It is a feeling of accomplishment," Calkins said. "I think there is a lot of history in this series now to be able to win the first event.

INDY RACING LEAGUE

"I had a car that could go anywhere on the race track."

And that allowed Buzz Calkins to drive all the way to victory lane.

Bruce Martin is the auto racing editor for United Press International and covers Indy car racing for National Speed Sport News.

15

Mission Accomplished

Tony George, founder of the Indy Racing League, wouldn't admit it but the president of the Indianapolis Motor Speedway had to feel a sense of "Mission Accomplished" after the unbelievably successful debut of his new racing series.

The script for the Jan. 27 Indy 200 at Walt Disney World could have come straight out of a Walt Disney movie: A man with strong convictions overcomes tremendous political adversity to endure in triumph in the end.

That man is Tony George. After experiencing some vicious political shots over his new, all-oval racing league, it would have been easy for George to give up and continue the status quo in Indy car racing. But he continued to fight and was able to enjoy the rewards of perseverance in the Indy 200 at Walt Disney World.

The grandstands were filled with 51,000 fans. Disney provided the pre-race entertainment in its usual spectacular fashion. And the fans witnessed a race that was competitive, featuring two young drivers who could pass themselves off as stars in a Disney feature film.

The race was won by 24-year-old Buzz Calkins, a graduate of the Indy Lights series. Finishing in second place was Tony Stewart, the first driver in racing history to win three national titles (Midget, Sprint and Silver Crown) in the same season in 1995.

The IRL was designed for drivers such as Stewart and Calkins — homegrown American talent who otherwise wouldn't have an opportunity to drive an Indy car.

Stewart was asked what his co-drivers in the midget and sprint car ranks might have thought after watching one of their own nearly win the Indy 200.

"I hope they are throwing a party for me right now," Stewart said. "I hope it opens up some team owners' eyes to some of the midget and sprint car drivers in USAC. I feel like open wheel drivers haven't had much of a chance lately and I hope with this finish it will help up open some doors for some of my fellow drivers."

But the most pleased individual at Disney World on Jan. 27 wasn't Mickey Mouse, it was Tony George. He saw his dream of a new series become a reality.

"I'm really proud of all these guys," George said. "They came out here and showed they are true professionals. All three of these young guys up here (Calkins, Stewart and third-place finisher Robbie Buhl), deserve a shot. That is what the IRL is all about. They got it and made the most of it and I couldn't be more pleased."

The success of the inaugural event buoyed George's thoughts on the rest of the season.

"We put on a good show," George said. "The fans enjoyed it, they enjoyed the entire weekend. There is fan support and sponsor support out there somewhere for what we are trying to do. I think the sponsors will see what took place here today and hopefully see it as an opportunity we are creating and will come and join us. It was fun."

George also recognizes after the display of talent by such USAC stars as Stewart, it will create renewed enthusiasm from USAC midget and sprint car drivers and fans.

"I know for the last several months a lot of those drivers have been talking about opportunity and it creates opportunity for them," George said. "We all know it is not going to be easy, but by seeing this today they feel they know there is still hope out there to one day have a dream to run in the Indianapolis 500 and one day fulfill it.

"That is where the real racing is. You know that."

So the Indy 200 at Walt Disney World proved to be a credible event. Although the depth of racing could not be termed great, the finish was very good and the event itself was outstanding, according to George and all those who witnessed the fanfare.

"I'm just really happy. I couldn't have been more pleased and I give it a 10."

More important than the rating was the fact the mission of launching the Indy Racing League had been accomplished.

DURA-LUBE 200

MARCH 24 1996

EVENT
REVIEW

INDY RACING LEAGUE

1 9 9 6 D U R A - L U B E 2 0 0

The Desert

By Bruce Martin

As the Indy Racing League moved to the "Jewel of the Desert", Buddy Jobe's fabulous 1.0-mile speedway in Phoenix, the series was gaining momentum. But the field that arrived at PIR was not short on experience as 15 of the 24 drivers who competed at Orlando had raced Indy cars at Phoenix with Roberto Guerrero and Arie Luyendyk. Seven more drivers had raced at Phoenix in other equipment, including Davey Hamilton, who had four wins in the Copper World Classic for super modified cars.

"This is going to be a fantastic group to race with," Hamilton said. "It has been something I have wanted to see happen for a long time. I've tried to get involved with Indy cars since 1988 and have tried to get a ride since 1991. It was just a dead-end street. I owe everything to the IRL. This is the reason Davey Hamilton is in an Indy car because this series is happening. It is great Buddy Jobe has a race at Phoenix International Raceway. I have a lot of great memories racing there.

"It is great to be in an Indy car now."

The Oldsmobile Aurora official pace car (above) led the field to the start of the 1996 Dura-Lube 200. Tony Stewart made a round of practice laps on the Desert Mile.

PHOENIX INTERNAT.

Heat........

Before pole qualifications began, however, three drivers were knocked out of the race with crashes in practice on Friday, March 22. Eddie Cheever, Stan Wattles and Buddy Lazier all crashed with Lazier suffering the most serious injury when he broke his pelvis and fractured one vertebra. Cheever was involved in the same crash and suffered a concussion while the third driver in that incident, Lyn St. James, was unhurt and able to compete in the race. Wattles was involved in a separate crash, suffering a concussion that kept him out of the event.

Lazier's injury was significant because he was the one of the fastest drivers in testing at Phoenix with a lap at 184.899 miles an hour in January. The only driver to run faster than Lazier at Phoenix was Richie Hearn's lap of 185.854 miles an hour on Feb. 28.

In a series filled with drivers that are new to Indy car racing, Luyendyk used his veteran experience to shatter the PIR track record by winning the pole. Luyendyk ran his 1995 Reynard/Ford-Cosworth to track record of

Rookie Richie Hearn burned up the track, nearly capturing the pole position.

IAL RACEWAY

After leading eleven laps, electrical problems forced Tony Stewart to park, finishing in 11th place.

183.599 mph. That broke the track record of 181.952 mph set by Bryan Herta in the 1994 CART race.

Hearn was the second fastest with a lap at 182.797 mph.

Capturing the pole boosted the confidence of 1990 Indy 500 winner Arie Luyendyk who lives in nearby Scottsdale, Ariz.

Luyendyk's qualification run came after Hearn had grabbed the pole.

"I'm not disappointed he outqualified me, I'm disappointed that I know the car is faster

Scott Sharp led 40 laps, finishing in second place, unable to defeat Luyendyk's commanding lead.

than the time showed," Hearn said. "Arie has been quick all week, too."

Roberto Guerrero, who won the Phoenix 200 in 1987, qualified third with a lap at 181.050 mph. He was followed by Stewart and 1995 Indianapolis 500 pole winner Scott Brayton.

On race day, Luyendyk once again showed the value of experience by taking the checkered flag. Luyendyk led the 200-lap race four times for 122 laps, including the final 66, to score his fourth career win in an Indy car. It was also his second career win at Phoenix.

"Someone said I'm an old fossil and that is why I'm sitting here today because experience really counts around these race tracks," Luyendyk said. "It is real easy to get into the wall and to get into trouble. You just have to be patient, work with your crew on the car and wait for the right time. That is what happened here today."

Luyendyk used that experience when he developed a loose condition with his race car on long runs following pit stops. But Luyendyk was able to maintain control of his car, and his composure, to beat Scott Sharp by 8.896 seconds. He averaged 117.368 miles an hour around the 1.0-mile oval in front of

32,000 fans.

"It is great to win again," Luyendyk said. "No matter what anybody says, what series we are running in, I'm still happy to run here. I'm committed to the IRL as is Fred Treadway, the car owner, and Jonathan Byrd as co-owner and sponsor with Bryant Heating and Cooling. Their main goal is to sponsor a race car in the Indianapolis 500 and now that the IRL has come about, they are now part of our group.

"I couldn't be happier for everybody involved."

Mike Groff was third followed by Hearn and Johnny O'Connell. Buzz Calkins was sixth after spinning out on the third lap.

With the first two IRL races completed, the series prepared to move on to Indianapolis for the month of May, culminating with the 80th Indianapolis 500.

"I enjoy Indy, so I'm going for the best deal that will help me win my second race there," Luyendyk said. "I know what it takes to win it. In my mind, I chose to be there. I'm certain there are a lot of other drivers who would like to be there, too.

"I don't get too excited about stuff, good or bad. I'm really happy. I'm very happy.

"I'm not going to sit here and cry for you, but I'm very happy."

Bruce Martin is the auto racing editor for United Press International and covers Indy car racing for National Speed Sport News.

Arie Luyendyk brought home the first ever victory for Jonathan Byrd.

Quest for the Dream

By
Bruce Martin

After winning an Indy car race for the first time as a team owner, Jonathan Byrd said this victory was for all the true oval racers who have died in quest of their dream.

"There are a few people I wish could have been here today," Byrd said after Arie Luyendyk drove to victory in the Dura-Lube 200 Indy Racing League event. "I wish Andy Kenopensky and Rich Vogler and Billy Vukovich, III and a few other guys could be around. It is a tremendous day.

"It is really a tremendous feeling. I've been trying for 12 years. Bryant Heating and Cooling has been with me for nine years. To be able to do this for sponsors who have been as loyal as they have been, Arie and I have been talking about getting together for a long time. It has finally come together."

Byrd has been a longtime supporter of the Indianapolis 500 and the United States Auto Club. The owner of the "World's Largest Cafeteria" in Greenwood, Ind. is the co-entrant of Luyendyk's car. Byrd joined forces with Vogler for the Indianapolis 500 from 1985-89. Byrd also served as the car owner for Vogler's USAC Midget team, sharing two national championships together.

Since 1985, Byrd has had five top-10 finishes in the Indianapolis 500, including sixth place Gordon Johncock in 1991 and another sixth by Scott Brayton in 1993.

In 1994, Byrd was a co-entrant with A.J. Foyt for driver John Andretti, who became the first driver in history to compete in both the Indianapolis 500 and the Coca-Cola 600 NASCAR Winston Cup race in the same day.

Prior to the 1996 IRL season, Byrd joined forces with Indianapolis businessman Fred Treadway to form a team for Arie Luyendyk, winner of the 1990 Indianapolis 500.

In just its second race, the team drove into victory lane.

The victory at Phoenix was also the first Indy car win for Bryant Heating and Cooling in 31 years of sponsorship, mostly with cars in the Indianapolis 500.

"Winning the Indianapolis 500 has been a lifelong goal," Byrd said. "Since 1985, I've been trying to win that. It won't mean less winning it

this year, if the Lord allows that to happen, than any other year to win the thing. There is going to be nobody in Indianapolis that is sorry they are driving there and I'm sure there are a lot of people who wish they were going to be driving at Indianapolis because Indianapolis is the race."

Jonathan Byrd believes after successfully staging the first two races, the Indy Racing League has arrived.

"There is no doubt the series has arrived when things like this race happen," Byrd said. "It is time now to stop talking about whether this series has arrived. It is here, it is real. Once we get our own cars and our own engines and don't have to do what we are doing now in putting these things together, this is going to be the premier series in auto sports.

An Indy car race on an oval track has a magic feeling to Byrd, which is why he is one of the IRL's strongest advocates.

"I'm a long-time oval track guy," Byrd said. "This series is everything I wanted to do to go oval track racing. That is where my heart is.

"This felt right today. That is what is so different, this really felt right. We are with people who really want to go oval racing and are racing for the sake of racing, not for all the other stuff, the politics that goes on. That is what Tony George is willing to sacrifice in order to bring back.

"And I'm with him."

The bottom line is, this was a victory for drivers like Vogler and Vukovich. That is the way Jonathan Byrd wants to remember his first win as a team owner.

"In 1990, we lost five people in one year. It was a tough year so this makes up for a lot of things. If it sounds like I was getting emotional about it, I was.

"It really is for them. Man, when you think IRL, does Rich Vogler come to mind? Was this thing made for him? That is not to take anything away from Arie because Arie is cut from the same cloth and that is why I wanted to be with him for so long. I'm just glad we were finally able to get the whole thing together."

EIGHTIETH INDIANAPOLIS 500

MAY 26, 1996

EVENT REVIEW

INDY RACING LEAGUE

ENTRY

Car No.	Driver	Car Name	Entrant	Year/Chassis/Engine/Tire
2	Scott Brayton	Glidden Menards Special	Team Menard, Inc.	95 Lola/Menard V6 /Firestone
3	Eddie Cheever	Quaker State Menards Special	Team Menard, Inc.	95 Lola/Menard V6 /Firestone
4	Richie Hearn	Della Penna Motorsports Ralph's Food 4 Less Fuji Film	Della Penna Motorsports	95 Reynard/Ford Cosworth V8/ Goodyear
5	Arie Luyendyk	Jonathan Byrd's Cafeteria/Bryant Heating & Cooling	Jonathan Byrd/Treadway Racing	95 Reynard/Ford Cosworth XB/Firestone
6	Buzz Calkins	Bradley Food Marts Reynard	Bradley Motorsports	TBA/Ford Cosworth XB/Firestone
7	Eliseo Salazar	Cristal/Copec Mobil	Team Scandia	95 Lola/Ford Cosworth V8/Goodyear
8	Fermin Velez	Alta Spring Water/Perry Ellis/ Royal Purple	Team Scandia	94 Lola/Ford Cosworth V8/Goodyear
9	Stephan Gregoire	Hemelgarn Racing	Hemelgarn Racing, Inc.	95 Reynard/Ford Cosworth XB/Firestone
10	TBA	Hemelgarn Racing	Hemelgarn Racing, Inc.	94 Reynard/Ford Cosworth XB/Firestone
11	Scott Sharp	Conseco AJ Foyt Racing	A J Foyt Enterprises	95 Lola/Ford Cosworth XB/Goodyear
12	Buzz Calkins	Bradley Food Marts/Reynard	Bradley Motorsports	95 Reynard/Ford Cosworth XB/Firestone
14	Davey Hamilton	AJ Foyt Copenhagen Racing	A J Foyt Enterprises	95 Lola/Ford Cosworth XB/Goodyear
15	David Kudrave	Tempero-Giuffre Racing	Tempero-Giuffre Racing	92 Lola/Buick V6/Goodyear
16	Johnny Parsons	Team Blueprint Racing Inc.	Team Blueprint Racing Inc.	93 Lola/Menard V6/Firestone
17	TBA	Leigh Miller Racing Lola Ford	Leigh Miller Racing	94 Lola/Ford Cosworth XB/Firestone
18	John Paul, Jr.	V-Line Earl's Supply	PDM Racing, Inc.	93 Lola/Menard V6/Goodyear
20	Tony Stewart	Menards/Glidden/Quaker State/ Special	Team Menard, Inc.	95 Lola/Menard V6/Firestone
21	Roberto Guerrero	WavePhore/Pennzoil Reynard-Ford	Pagan Racing	95 Reynard/Ford Cosworth V8/Goodyear
22	Michel Jourdain, Jr.	Herdez Quaker State Canels	Team Scandia	95 Lola/Ford Cosworth V8/Goodyear
23	Tony Stewart	Menards/Glidden/Quaker State/ Special	Team Menard, Inc.	95 Lola/Menard V6/Firestone
24	Randy Tolsma	McCormack Motorsports	McCormack Motorsports	93 Lola/TBA/TBA
25	TBA	Tempero-Giuffre Racing	Tempero-Giuffre Racing	92 Lola/TBA/Goodyear
27	Jim Guthrie	Team Blueprint Racing Inc.	Team Blueprint Racing Inc.	93 Lola/Menard V6/Firestone
28	TBA	Automatic Fire Sprinklers	PDM Racing, Inc.	95 Lola/Ford Cosworth V8/Goodyear
29	TBA	Slick Gardner/Indy Project	Slick Gardner/Indy Project	92 Lola/Ford Cosworth XB/TBA
30	Eddie Cheever	Quaker State Menards Special	Team Menard, Inc.	95 Lola/Menard V6/Firestone
31	Randy Tolsma	McCormack Motorsports	McCormack Motorsports	93 Lola/TBA/TBA
32	Danny Ongais	Glidden Menards Special	Team Menard, Inc.	95 Lola/Menard V6/Firestone
33	Michele Alboreto	Alta Spring Water/Perry Ellis/ Royal Purple	Team Scandia	95 Reynard/Ford Cosworth V8/Goodyear
34	Eliseo Salazar	Cristal/Copec Mobil	Team Scandia	95 Lola/Ford Cosworth V8/Goodyear
35	TBA	Treadway Racing	Treadway Racing	95 Reynard/Ford Cosworth XB/Firestone
36	Dan Drinan	Loop Hole Racing	Loop Hole Racing	91 Lola/Buick V6/Goodyear
37	TBA	Leigh Miller Racing Lola Ford	Leigh Miller Racing	94 Lola/Ford Cosworth XB/Firestone
38	TBA	PDM Racing, Inc./ Leigh Miller Racing	PDM Racing, Inc./ Leigh Miller Racing	94 Lola/Ford Cosworth V8/Goodyear
39	Scott Harrington	Harrington Motorsports/ LP Racing	Harrington Motorsports/ LP Racing	92 Lola/Buick V6/TBA
40	TBA	Arizona Executive Air	Arizona Motor Sport Racing	93 Lola/TBA/TBA
41	TBA	A J Foyt Enterprises	A J Foyt Enterprises	94 Lola/Ford Cosworth XB/Goodyear
43	TBA	Alta Spring Water/Perry Ellis/ Royal Purple	Team Scandia	94 Lola/Ford Cosworth V8/Goodyear

Car No.	Driver	Car Name	Entrant	Year/Chassis/Engine/Tire
44	Richie Hearn	Della Penna Motorsports Ralph's Food 4 Less Fuji Film	Della Penna Motorsports	95 Reynard/Ford Cosworth V8/Goodyear
45	TBA	Spirit of San Antonio	Zunne' Group Racing	94 Lola/ Ford Cosworth XB/Firestone
46	Johnny Unser	Ruger-Titanium/Project Indy/Reynard	Project Indy	93 Lola/Ford Cosworth XB/Goodyear
48	TBA	A J Foyt Enterprises	A J Foyt Enterprises	94 Lola/Ford Cosworth XB/Goodyear
50	Russ Wicks	Gibson Musical Instruments	Osella USA Inc.	95 Reynard/Ford Cosworth XB/TBA
52	Robbie Buhl	Beck Motorsports	Beck Motorsports	94 Lola/Ford Cosworth XB/Firestone
53	Mark Dismore	Menards Special	Team Menard, Inc.	93 Lola/Menard V6/Firestone
54	Robbie Buhl	Beck Motorsports	Beck Motorsports	94 Lola/Ford Cosworth XB/Firestone
55	Russ Wicks	Gibson Musical Instruments	Osella USA Inc.	95 Reynard/Ford Cosworth XB/TBA
59	TBA	Hemelgarn Racing	Hemelgarn Racing Inc.	94 Reynard/TBA/Firestone
60	Mike Groff	Valvoline Cummins Craftsman Special	Walker Racing	95 Reynard/Ford Cosworth XB/Goodyear
62	TBA	Menards Special	Team Menard, Inc.	93 Lola/Menard V6/Firestone
63	Michele Alboreto	Alta Spring Water/Perry Ellis/ Royal Purple	Team Scandia	95 Lola/Ford Cosworth V8/Goodyear
64	Johnny Unser	Ruger-Titanium/Project Indy/Reynard	Project Indy	95 Reynard/Ford Cosworth XB/Goodyear
65	TBA	Tempero-Giuffre Racing	Tempero-Giuffre Racing	93 Lola/TBA/Goodyear
66	Jeff Wood	Burns Motorsports, Inc.	Burns Motorsports, Inc.	92 Lola/Buick V6/TBA
68	TBA	Burns Motorsports, Inc.	Burns Motorsports, Inc.	92 Lola/Buick V6/TBA
70	Davy Jones	Delco Electronics High Tech Team Galles	Galles Racing International	95 Lola/Mercedes Ilmor/Goodyear
72	Davy Jones	Delco Electronics High Tech Team Galles	Galles Racing International	95 Lola/Mercedes Ilmor/Goodyear
73	Michel Jourdain, Jr.	Herdez Quaker State Canels	Team Scandia	95 Lola/Ford Cosworth V8/Goodyear
75	Johnny O'Connell	Cunningham Racing	Cunningham Racing	95 Reynard/Ford Cosworth XB/Firestone
77	Butch Brickell	Brickell Racing Group	Butch Brickell	93 Lola/Menard V6/Goodyear
79	Scott Harrington	Harrington Motorsports/LP Racing	Harrington Motorsports/LP Racing	92 Lola/TBA/TBA
80	TBA	Arizona Executive Air	Arizona Motor Sport Racing	92 Lola/TBA/TBA
82	TBA	A J Foyt Enterprises	A J Foyt Enterprises	93 Lola/Ford Cosworth XB/Goodyear
84	TBA	A J Foyt Enterprises	A J Foyt Enterprises	94 Lola/Ford Cosworth XB/Goodyear
85	TBA	Spirit of San Antonio	Zunne' Group Racing	TBA/TBA/TBA
87	TBA	Pagan Racing	Pagan Racing	92 Lola/Buick V6/Goodyear
88	TBA	Average Joe's Sports Pub & Grub	Treadway Racing	94 Reynard/Ford Cosworth XB/Firestone
89	TBA	Hemelgarn Racing	Hemelgarn Racing, Inc.	92 Lola/TBA/Firestone
90	Lyn St. James	Lifetime TV/Alta Water/ Perry Ellis/Royal Purple	Team Scandia	94 Lola/Ford Cosworth V8/Goodyear
91	Buddy Lazier	Hemelgarn Racing-Delta Faucet	Hemelgarn Racing, Inc.	95 Reynard/Ford Cosworth XB/Firestone
92	Brad Murphey	Hemelgarn Racing	Hemelgarn Racing, Inc.	92 Lola/Buick V6/Firestone
93	Fermin Velez	Alta Spring Water/Perry Ellis/ Royal Purple	Team Scandia	94 Lola/Ford Cosworth V8/Goodyear
94	Hideshi Matsuda	Beck Motorsports	Beck Motorsports	95 Lola/Ford Cosworth XB/Firestone
95	Hideshi Matsuda	Beck Motorsports	Beck Motorsports	94 Lola/Ford Coswroth XB/Firestone
96	Paul Durant	ABF Motorsports USA Sunrise Rental Canada	ABF Motorsports LLC	92 Lola/Buick V6/Goodyear
98	Roberto Guerrero	WavePhore/Pennzoil Reynard-Ford	Pagan Racing	95 Reynard/Ford Cosworth V8/Goodyear
99	TBA	Pagan Racing	Pagan Racing	94 Reynard/Ford Cosworth V8/Goodyear

The following chronology of the month of May, 1996, was written by Jan Shaffer, Trackside Report editor for the Speedway. The information was compiled under the direction of Bob Walters, IMS Director of Public Relations.

Contributing to this chronicle as the month of May unfolded were Speedway Press Room Manager Bill York and staffers Bob Clidinst, Tim Sullivan, Josh Laycock, Jack Marsh and Bob Wilson; public relations assistant Amy Riley; the Trackside Report team of assistants Lisa Sommers, Janine Vogrin, Becky Lenhard and Vern Morseman and staffers Ty Cheatum, Sandye Gier, Ruth Ann Cadou Hofmann, Tony Hofmann, Renee Lane, Al Larsen, Suzanne Robinson, Starre Szelag and historian Bob Watson; and Speedway Director of Computer Resources Lee Driggers and assistants Kris Callfas, Jeremy Lane, Richard Smith and Sue Watson.

The 1996 Trackside Report was dedicated to the memory of Bob Laycock (1914-1995), the longtime Indianapolis Motor Speedway historian. Bob's unparalleled knowledge of the Indianapolis 500, his contributions to the information system, the Speedway family, the racing community and the history of the sport will be greatly missed.

The track opening for practice for the 80th running of the Indianapolis 500 had a different flavor.

For the first time, the United States Auto Club's Rookie Orientation Program was part of the start of the storied month of May and the group of newcomers prepared to take their chance at history was a big one.

But rain descended throughout the morning and opening ceremonies were moved to a hospitality tent, where Bud Liebler of Chrysler presented the keys to the 1996 Dodge Viper GTS pace car to Speedway President Tony George.

George presented the keys to USAC Chief Steward Keith Ward, who took over the helm from the retired Tom Binford, signifying the opening of the track.

However, the rain had something to say about it, and Ward closed the track for the day at 3:50 p.m. with nary a lap turned. It was the second opening-day rainout at the Speedway in three years.

But everyone knew that the sun would shine. A total of 29 drivers had passed physi-

QUOTE OF THE DAY:
"Now go, if you can."

cal exams and 34 drivers had attended a meeting for rookie drivers the previous day. Twenty-two cars were on the grounds and seven had already passed technical inspection.

On this day, research by USAC steward John Notte revealed that oval-track racing was celebrating its centennial season.

Notte's research showed the first oval-track race was held Sept. 7, 1896 at Narragansett Race Park in Providence, R.I. It was a five-lap race on a one-mile oval with seven cars. The winning time was 15 minutes, one second. It was won by one of two Riker-Electrics. The other five cars were Duryeas. Reportedly, 50,000 people attended.

It was ironic that the starting command was, "Now go, if you can."

On this day at Indianapolis, just short of 100 years later, nobody could.

Above: Rain forced Team Foyt back into their garage. Left: IMS President Tony George accepted the Dodge Viper GTS pace car keys from Bud Liebler of Chrysler.

Date:	Saturday, May 4
Weather:	Rain, High 62°
Drivers On Track:	0
Cars On Track:	0
Total Laps:	0

Because of the opening-day washout, all the "firsts" of the month occurred on this day.

The #15 Tempero-Giuffre car assigned to rookie Justin Bell was the first to pit road. Rookie Jim Guthrie was the first driver in uniform on pit road. Mark Dismore was the first to saddle up. Team Menard crewman Scott Parks was the first to fire an engine, doing so for Tony Stewart's car.

Michele Alboreto was the first to leave pit road. Stewart was the first to complete a lap. Dismore was the first to pass a phase of his driver's test.

Dismore was the first to complete two phases and Stewart and Buzz Calkins passed their first phases.

And then it rained again. Parks' firing of Stewart's engine to the track's closing took just 37 minutes. Nine cars had been on the track during the period. Teams and drivers waited for better weather throughout the day, but USAC Chief Steward Keith Ward made the closing official at 3:30 p.m.

The rain didn't deter the 16th annual "Save Arnold" Barbecue for Special Olympics of Indiana, although the sports exhibition portion was canceled.

The event was moved to a hospitality tent, where the group watched the Indiana Pacers on television — until a group of drivers, grounded by the weather, arrived to stage an impromptu autograph session. A total of 29 current and former drivers participated.

More than $75,000 was raised for Special Olympics of Indiana as the event's all-time contributions total reached $1.3 million.

"I think it's wonderful these guys have taken the time to sit down and do this," said Speedway Chairman Mari Hulman George, who initiated the event in 1981 and has hosted it each year.

At least one driver missed the sports exhibition part, in which drivers and celebrities are matched with Special Olympians.

"Last year it was baseball," said Alessandro Zampedri, with a smile. "This year it was going to be basketball and I'm pretty good at that."

This team took advantage of another rainy day by spending time in the garage to fine tune their machine.

Date:	Sunday, May 5
Weather:	Windy, High 69°
Drivers On Track:	9
Cars On Track:	9
Total Laps:	138

Top Five Drivers of the Day

Car	Driver	Speed
20	Tony Stewart	193.957
23	Mark Dismore	193.569
33	Michele Alboreto	188.648
44	Richie Hearn	188.415
12	Buzz Calkins	188.233

QUOTE OF THE DAY:
"It's like a Cadillac." — Tony Stewart

Tony Stewart greeted the crowd at the first annual Race Rock'n Roll Party, held in downtown Indy at Monument Circle.

As bad weather took a raincheck, a flurry of activity took place as 11 drivers breezed through the rookie test and Tony Stewart reeled off a new set of records.

Stewart was given an early green light by officials and showed the rest the short way around the 2 1/2-mile oval.

According to Team Menard director of racing Larry Curry, the lap came after a USAC official told Curry that Stewart could run at any comfortable speed.

"Don't just tell me to go out there, or I will (meaning Stewart)," Curry responded.

So Stewart did. "Comfortable" meant 231.774 miles per hour in the #20 Menards/Glidden/Quaker State Special, the fastest lap for a rookie in Speedway history.

Later in the day, Stewart cranked out a lap at 237.336, the fastest practice lap in Speedway history, breaking the mark of 234.913 set by Arie Luyendyk on May 12, 1995. Stewart's trap speed was a whopping 244.

"It was the first day we really got to let it go and it's fast," Stewart said. "We trimmed it out a little from this morning and I ran it flat all the way around.

"When I was out there, Larry called in and said, 'Pit, pit, pit' and I radioed back and said, 'What's wrong?', And he said, 'Nothing. You just were really fast.'

"I told Larry the car felt more comfortable at 237 than 231. It's like a Cadillac. It's an honor to have the fastest lap."

Stewart's boxcar numbers opened the door to questions about where the limit might be. By the end of the day, he had become the fifth driver in Speedway history to exceed 230 miles per hour in two different cars on the same day.

"I've had people ask me if I think 240 is doable and this guy sitting next to me (Stewart) thinks there's more left in the car, so we'll see," Curry said.

Mark Dismore was the fastest to complete the driver's test, getting the "all clear" in just 71 minutes. Stewart took five minutes longer.

Michele Alboreto, Buzz Calkins, Michel Jourdain Jr. and Richie Hearn all completed the test in the morning runs. Racin Gardner, Randy Tolsma, Dan Drinan, Brad Murphey and Jim Guthrie finished in the day's final hour. Paul Durant and Johnny Unser each passed two phases and Fermin Velez got his first phase done.

Completing the test was particularly rewarding for Dismore, a resident of nearby Greenfield who returned to the Speedway after a serious accident years earlier.

"I can understand why the foreign guys want to come over here and run," Dismore said. "This place is really special."

"We just went out there and tried to run it comfortably," said Calkins. "Hopefully, we can test under normal conditions and start running fast again."

Meanwhile, Tiara Motor Coach Corporation and Stihl were announced as new official sponsors of the Speedway. A steady stream of driver visitors to the Hanna Medical Center upped the list of those passing the driver physical to 47. A total of 36 cars were now on hand.

And the veterans were waiting to get on the track.

Date:	Monday, May 6	
Weather:	Cloudy, High 62°	
Drivers On Track:	10	
Cars On Track:	10	
Total Laps:	313	

Top Five Drivers of the Day

Car	Driver	Speed
20	Tony Stewart	237.336
30	Mark Dismore	228.566
22	Michel Jourdain Jr.	228.154
12	Buzz Calkins	227.411
44	Richie Hearn	226.592

As the veterans got their first taste of the month of May, 1996, it became obvious that records would go out the window.

It was the first day that the battle began to take shape. The shootout for the pole would be between Arie Luyendyk and the three Team Menard drivers — Scott Brayton, Eddie Cheever and Tony Stewart.

Indeed, people started talking about "Arie and the Menards".

The Menards got the best of the rest on this day, with Stewart taking the top spot on the speed ladder on a lap at 236.121 miles per hour in the #20 Menards/Glidden/Quaker State Special. Cheever was next at 235.997, chalked up in the day's final minute in the #3 Quaker State Menards Special. Brayton was third at 235.750 in the #2 Glidden Menards Special, followed by Luyendyk at 233.621 in the #5 Jonathan Byrd's Cafeteria/Bryant Heating & Cooling entry.

The day also involved a close call when Stewart almost collided with fellow rookie Brad Murphey while trying to pass.

"I caught Brad on the backstretch and thought I could get by him," Stewart said. "I just tried to go underneath him. It was just a learning experience. I won't do that again."

Brayton, the defending pole winner, praised the track surface.

"This is the smoothest, without a doubt, that the track has ever been," he said. "If you'd been here before and came back now, it's incredibly smooth and has a lot of grip. It's going to take us places we haven't been yet."

"...and don't want to go," Cheever chimed in. "I'm almost embarrassed to be running this good so early."

Roberto Guerrero and Buzz Calkins also cleared the 230-mile-per-hour barrier and Scott Sharp and Richie Hearn were knocking on the door with 229-pluses.

Johnny Unser and Paul Durant became the 12th and 13th drivers to pass the driver's test.

Zunne Group Racing announced that Lyn St. James would drive its entry, the #45 Spirit of San Antonio machine, to be fielded by McCormack Motorsports.

"I'm very proud that this is my first Indy car ride that's not predicated on sponsorships," St. James said.

It was also learned that Stan Wattles, who led the Indy Racing League's inaugural event at Walt Disney World, and his wife Jill became the parents of Caroline Alexandra the previous day.

"We've already got Caroline's go-kart picked out," Wattles said, after sending a box of fine cigars to the Speedway press room.

Twenty-three cars found their way onto the track, and after the day's running, 33 drivers had practiced in the first four days.

And Danny Ongais passed his physical at the track's Hanna Medical Center, bringing back memories of the "Flyin' Hawaiian" of years past.

Three days remained before the pole position would be decided.

QUOTE OF THE DAY:
"I won't do that again."
— Tony Stewart

Rookie Richie Hearn pleased some young fans with his autograph.

Date:	Tuesday, May 7
Weather:	Rain, High 63°
Drivers On Track:	20
Cars On Track:	23
Total Laps:	754

Top Five Drivers of the Day

Car	Driver	Speed
20	Tony Stewart	236.121
3	Eddie Cheever	235.997
2	Scott Brayton	235.750
5	Arie Luyendyk	233.621
21	Roberto Guerrero	232.336

QUOTE OF THE DAY:
"He loved the place."
— *Larry Davidson*

Team Menard had to keep their mounts in the stable due to another day of wet weather.

Just when the march toward Pole Day was getting started in earnest, rain struck again and USAC Chief Steward Keith Ward called it quits at 2:35 p.m. without a lap being turned.

The day was to be the annual USAC Promoter's Day, in which USAC race organizers from around the country attend the track's activities. They saw very little.

That left it as a day of reflection and remembrance of two who were absent during this month of May.

The Speedway had started the month for the first time in more than 40 years without Speedway historian Bob Laycock manning the front office of the press room. Mr. Laycock had died at the age of 81 six months prior to the 80th month of May. With the exception of the 1995 race, he had attended every Indianapolis 500 since he was born.

His grandson, Josh, son of Bob Laycock Jr., had joined the press-room staff on Opening Day and assumed some of the press room's historical and detail duties long associated with the family name.

Another familiar figure was also absent. Don Hutson, a fireman at the Speedway since 1965, had passed on a month earlier after a long illness. His most recent assignment was driving the Turn 2 safety truck. At his request, he was buried in a Speedway firesuit.

"He loved the place and lived for the place," said Larry Davidson, an equipment coordinator for the Speedway fire crew.

A small, baseball-card size magnetized photo of Hutson was mounted behind the driver's door on each of the track's 14 fire trucks for the month. And a sign was hung from the fence near the Turn 2 fire truck station.

It read: "In Memory of Don Hutson, Fireman & Friend. Turn 2 won't be the same without you."

A total of 45 cars were now at the track and only two days of practice — barring rain — remained before the pole position for the Indianapolis 500 was to be decided.

Date:	Wednesday, May 8
Weather:	Rain, High 66°
Drivers On Track:	0
Cars On Track:	0
Total Laps:	0

QUOTE OF THE DAY:
"I was a little surprised."
— *Arie Luyendyk*

The roles were reversed on this day from Day 4 in the "Arie and the Menards" story of speed.

Arie Luyendyk let it be known that the Team Menard drivers Tony Stewart, Scott Brayton and Eddie Cheever wouldn't have a "gimme" for the pole.

Luyendyk's sixth and seventh laps of the day were 231.071 miles per hour and 232.007 in the #5 Jonathan Byrd's Cafeteria/Bryant Heating & Cooling entry, letting everyone know that there was more to come.

The Menard drivers, Scott Sharp and Buddy Lazier challenged, but fell short as the day wore on.

At 4:20 p.m., Luyendyk upped the ante, running the fastest three practice laps in Speedway history consecutively at 237.505, 237.712 and 237.774. This time, it was in the #35 Treadway Racing team car.

Stewart turned a lap of 237.029 in the #20 Menards/Glidden/Quaker State Special just 57 minutes before the track closed, but it was clearly Luyendyk's turn at the front.

"I was a little surprised going that quickly," Luyendyk said. "I went 233 in my primary car, then jumped four miles an hour in this one. I wasn't flat all the way around. Turns 3 and 4 aren't much of a problem but Turns 1 and 2 are problems today.

"I had to turn a lot because of the wind. It wasn't comfortable or an easy ride but this car handles really well. It has the same setup as the other one and I don't know why it goes faster. This car is 'freer' in the corners. It doesn't scrub off as much.

"We haven't given up on our primary car, but there's a definite possibility that we'll use this one. I think 240 is quite possible. All you need is an engine with 10 more horsepower and one-tenth of an inch of boost. And, of course, the weather helps, too."

Luyendyk's fast laps broke a Team Menard streak. Team Menard cars had led the speed chart on nine consecutive practice days before Pole Day going back to 1995.

Robbie Buhl and Tyce Carlson each passed four phases of the driver's test and Joe Gosek passed the first two phases.

Meanwhile, Speedway President Tony George held a national teleconference in the Trackside Conference Room. He said the field would be full and hinted at the possibility of adding cars past the traditional 33.

"Certainly the sport itself is in transition," George said. "There are a lot of new names. There's been a very warm reception in this community for the drivers who are here. I feel very strongly that this is a unique year, an unusual year in all respects.

"We have 45 cars on the grounds so far and 40 have been through technical inspection," he added. "All indications are that the equipment is capable of attaining acceptable speeds. I don't believe the traditional 33 starting spots will be a problem to fill.

"The question is, will we consider expanding it in trying to show appreciation for the support of the IRL teams? Our minds are open to any number of things. The possibility is always there to expand beyond 33. We started 35 in recent history (1979)."

Thirty-two cars ran a total of 1,444 laps as the assault on speed for the pole position carried onward. Eight drivers had exceeded 230 miles per hour.

One more day of fast practice remained.

Rookie driver Tyce Carlson (left) received a few pointers from veteran John Paul, Jr.

Date:	Thursday, May 9
Weather:	Rain, High 77°
Drivers On Track:	32
Cars On Track:	32
Total Laps:	1,444

Top Five Drivers of the Day

Car	Driver	Speed
35	Arie Luyendyk	237.774
20	Tony Stewart	237.029
2	Scott Brayton	234.070
3	Eddie Cheever	234.034
91	Buddy Lazier	233.161

Scott Sharp

Long-time voice of the Speedway Tom Carnegie (right) chatted with "The Flying Dutchman" Arie Luyendyk about predicted pole speeds.

For the second straight day, Arie Luyendyk pushed the envelope even further after a cat-and-mouse game with the drivers of Team Menard.

The chronology of speed told the tale of "Fast Friday."

Scott Brayton turned a lap at 235.270 miles per hour in the #2 Glidden/Menards Special just five minutes into practice. A few minutes later, he upped it to 235.688. Then came Menard teammate Tony Stewart at 236.004 in the #20 Menards/Glidden/Quaker State Special.

Luyendyk went out and turned a lap at 236.992 in the #35 Treadway Racing entry just 18 minutes after Stewart's hot circuit to take command for the day. Others shot at this number to no avail.

At 12:29 p.m., Luyendyk put the icing on the cake with a lap at 238.045, fastest practice lap in Speedway history. Thirty-five minutes later, he capped it off with a lap at 239.260. Both laps came in the #35 "back-up" machine.

"I definitely had a pretty good tow on that lap," Luyendyk said of his fastest effort. "It was a black car...I don't know who it was, maybe John Paul Jr. The lap looked good on paper, though.

"I'd really like to get the pole," he added. "Last year, I had a pretty good shot at it but it didn't happen. This year, we have a one-car team and have a really good shot. I think we can put two laps in the 237 range. Speed fluctuates. The first lap is never as fast but we can probably end up in the 237 range. You only want to run as fast as you have to go in my mind."

In addition to Luyendyk's effort, it was clearly the fastest practice day of the month, with all drivers in the top 10 exceeding 231 miles per hour.

Scott Sharp was third on the list behind Stewart with a lap at 235.701 in the #11 Conseco AJ Foyt Racing machine. Buzz Calkins and Buddy Lazier were in the 234 mile-per-hour bracket.

Robbie Buhl completed the observation phase of his driver's test to become the 14th rookie cleared to drive.

Off the track, it was a day of announcements.

Calkins picked up sponsorship for his Bradley Motorsports entry from the Hoosier Lottery. LANCO International and Mi-Jack Products announced sponsorship of Alessandro Zampedri's Team Scandia ride.

ABC Sports announced that the network's long broadcasting relationship with the Indianapolis Motor Speedway would be extended through 1999.

Pennzoil, which became Official Motor Oil of the Speedway earlier in the year, announced it had 19 cars contracted to use its motor oil in the "500."

The pole awaited.

Tony Stewart prepared to catch up with Luyendyk's 239 mark, coming in at 236 mph for the day.

Date:	Friday, May 10	
Weather:	Windy, High 73°	
Drivers On Track:	29	
Cars On Track:	29	
Total Laps:	685	

Top Five Drivers of the Day

Car	Driver	Speed
35	Arie Luyendyk	239.260
20	Tony Stewart	236.004
11	Scott Sharp	235.701
2	Scott Brayton	235.688
12	Buzz Calkins	234.693

Above: Four-time Indy 500 starter Davy Jones qualified at 232.882, good for a front row starting spot, his career best. Right: It was a familiar sight this month of May to see safety crews working to dry the track.

The day started with Johnny O'Connell getting a sponsor and ended with Scott Brayton picking up his second straight Indianapolis 500 pole. But everything that happened in between —and after — gave race fans a memorable Pole Day.

O'Connell and Cunningham Racing announced in the morning that Mechanics Laundry had come on board to sponsor their effort. After that, speed came to some and problems came to others.

Johnny Parsons was the first to encounter the latter category when he hit the Turn 3 wall at 11:58 a.m. Parsons suffered a bruised left foot but the #16 Team Blueprint Racing entry sustained heavy left-side and rear-end damage.

Arie Luyendyk was practicing at the time and put two wheels on the grass to avoid a wayward tire from Parsons' car. Less than a half hour later, Luyendyk had problems of his own, requiring a tow-in for an engine problem that would delay his qualifying effort.

The A.J. Foyt stable was hit hard, both Marco Greco and Scott Sharp parked for engine changes.

For some, the speed was there.

Buzz Calkins reached 233.973 miles per hour in the #12 Bradley Food Marts Reynard, Eddie Cheever got up to 233.876 in the #3 Quaker State Menards Special and Tony Stewart topped the chart with a lap of 235.719 in the #20 Menards/Glidden/Quaker State Special.

Wet conditions early in the morning had delayed practice and qualifying didn't start until 2 p.m.

Lyn St. James was "first up" and qualified

QUOTE OF THE DAY:
"I was huntin' and lookin'."
— *Scott Brayton*

the #45 Spirit of San Antonio machine at a four-lap average of 224.594. She became the first female driver ever to hold the pole for the Indianapolis 500, but it was short-lived as Buddy Lazier reeled off a four-lap run of 231.468 just five minutes later in the #91 Hemelgarn Racing-Delta Faucet entry.

Johnny Unser became the first rookie to lock in a spot in the starting lineup with a four-lap average of 226.115 in the Ruger-Titanium/Project Indy/Reynard.

Alessandro Zampedri became the fourth qualifier with a run of 229.595 in the #8 Mi-Jack/AGIP/Dinema entry, second fastest at that point.

Then came Davy Jones. The veteran driver took the #70 Delco Electronics High Tech Team Galles machine to a one-lap track record of 233.064 and a new four-lap mark of 232.882. Roberto Guerrero's records of 232.618 for one lap and 232.482 for four laps had lasted for four years.

Mike Groff was next, and put together a run of 228.704 in the #60 Valvoline Cummins Craftsman Special.

Richie Hearn then put his name in the Speedway's record books. He fashioned a run of 226.521, a four-lap qualifying record for a rookie, in the #4 Della Penna Motorsports Ralph's Food 4 Less Fuji Film car.

His record, too, lasted only five minutes as Tony Stewart knocked Jones off the pole with a one-lap record of 233.179 and a four-lap average of 233.100 in the #20 Menards/ Glidden/Quaker State Special. Stewart

became the first rookie to set both one- and four-lap standards since Teo Fabi in 1983.

After John Paul Jr. waved off, Buzz Calkins qualified at 229.013 in the #12 Bradley Food Marts Reynard.

Jim Guthrie averaged 222.394 in the #27 Team Blueprint Racing car for a locked-in position, but the slowest of 10 qualifiers to this point.

Davey Hamilton put away his qualifying experience of a year earlier to make his first "500" field at 228.887 in the #14 AJ Foyt Copenhagen Racing machine.

Then came a major barrage of speed, starting with Eddie Cheever's run at 231.781 in the #3 Quaker State Menards Special. Roberto Guerrero was next at 231.373 in the #21 WavePhore/Pennzoil Reynard-Ford.

After Michele Alboreto waved off, Eliseo Salazar put together a run of 232.684 in the #34 Cristal/Copec/Mobil machine and Scott Brayton reached 231.535 in the #2 Glidden Menards Special.

All, however, fell short of Stewart's run and the young lion remained on the pole.

Michel Jourdain Jr., was next, and became the field's second-fastest rookie at 229.380 in the #22 Herdex Quaker State Canels machine.

Stephan Gregoire and Mark Dismore joined the field before the qualifying line broke for those who wanted to wait until day's end. Gregoire qualified the #9 Hemelgarn Racing machine at 227.556 and Dismore became the fourth driver for Team Menard to make the show, staging a four-lap run of 227.260 in the #30 Quaker State Menards Special.

Michele Alboreto and John Paul Jr. became the 19th and 20th qualifiers before "Happy Hour." Alboreto, on his second

Above: Pole Day for Johnny Parsons ended in an encounter with the turn #3 wall, causing a minor injury to his foot but extensive damage to his car.

Richie Hearn

Above: Scott Brayton posed for his second consecutive Pole qualifying picture. Right: Tony Stewart had high hopes for the Pole, yet wasn't disappointed with his speed of 233.100 mph.

attempt, checked in at 228.229 in the #33 Alta Spring Water/Perry Ellis/Royal Purple entry and Paul Jr. reached 224.757 in the V-Line Earl's Supply machine, also on a second attempt.

At 5:27 p.m., Luyendyk rolled away for his run in the #35 Jonathan Byrd's Cafeteria/Bryant Heating & Cooling car. After a first lap of 231.756, the 1990 winner found speed and set a one-lap record of 234.742 and a four-lap record of 233.390 to drop Stewart from the coveted No. 1 spot.

While he was on his run, however, Team Menard was in strategy. Word drifted out of the garage that if Luyendyk took the pole from Stewart, owner John Menard and Larry Curry, his chief strategist, would roll out a backup car in an attempt to retake the pole.

The Menard team had four drivers in the field — Stewart, Eddie Cheever, Mark Dismore and Scott Brayton. The pit lane was abuzz. It would be Brayton, the defending pole winner, who would get the call.

It didn't take long. Just 13 minutes after Luyendyk's run, Team Menard withdrew Brayton's qualified car from its second-row spot in the starting lineup and pushed the #32 Glidden Menards Special in line. Ironically, it was the same car that Luyendyk had qualified for the team a year earlier.

Two minutes later, at 5:42 p.m., Brayton was saddled up and on the move. His laps of 233.675, 233.536, 233.809 and 233.851 averaged 233.718. The four-lap average beat Luyendyk's track record and knocked him off the pole by just .328 of a mile per hour.

Although Scott Sharp started a final run and waved off, Brayton had stolen the pole. A wave of emotion swept through the Menard team.

"Nothing is more exciting than the Indianapolis Motor Speedway on Pole Day," Brayton said. "The Indy 500 is what Indy car racing is. I used to listen to Sid Collins when I was four and wanted to come to this place. There are a lot of people who love this place.

"The last two laps, I was huntin' and lookin' for any speed because I figured I needed a 234. I tried to keep it as free as it could be. To put it in the field and be happy, but disappointed because you're not on the front row...then come back a couple hours later and have all that change...this is the most emotion I've ever been through."

As Team Menard celebrated, another

drama developed. Luyendyk's car was found to be seven pounds under weight in technical inspection and his run was disallowed. He would be required to requalify and his one-lap mark of 234.742 was stricken from the record books. The one-lap mark reverted to Brayton's fastest lap.

"The car went through last night and it was five pounds too heavy," Luyendyk said. "We were okay there. Then we broke an engine and then the second engine, something went wrong. I'm not sure. Embarrassed may be a big word. We didn't do it intentionally. This has put a damper on things. The fact that I got put off the pole...I could have gotten over

Left: Arie Luyendyk's one-lap record of 234.742 was stricken after his car was found to be underweight. Above: Team Menard's gamble to get the pole paid off to the tune of $100,000.

that tomorrow. The guys worked their butts off today and because they did, there's an oversight."

Brayton became the ninth driver in history to claim back-to-back poles. Stewart's start on the front row was the first for a rookie since Teo Fabi started on the 1983 pole. Seven rookies bettered Andre Ribeiro's year-old rookie track record.

As it turned out, all three front-row qualifiers — Jones, Stewart and Brayton — set one- and four-lap track records when their turns came. And, with Luyendyk still not qualified and on a mission, more record-breaking could come.

	Date:	Saturday, May 11
	Weather:	Sunny, High 61°
Qualification Attempts:		25
Qualifiers:		21

Pole Day Qualifiers

Car	Driver	Speed
32	Scott Brayton	233.718
35	Arie Luyendyk	233.390
20	Tony Stewart	233.100
70	Davy Jones	232.882
34	Eliseo Salazar	232.716
3	Eddie Cheever	231.781
2	Scott Brayton (Withdrawn)	231.535
91	Buddy Lazier	231.468
21	Roberto Guerrero	231.373
8	Alessandro Zampedri	229.595
22	Michel Jourdain Jr.	229.380
12	Buzz Calkins	229.013
14	Davey Hamilton	228.887
60	Mike Groff	228.704
33	Michele Alboreto	228.229
9	Stephan Gregoire	227.556
30	Mark Dismore	227.260
4	Richie Hearn	226.521
64	Johnny Unser	226.115
18	John Paul Jr.	224.757
45	Lyn St. James	224.594
27	Jim Guthrie	222.394

Sunday proved to be a better day for Luyendyk (right, ABC's Gary Gerould left) as he bested Brayton's record Pole speed from the day before by more than 3 mph.

real mother of a day.

"I didn't sleep well last night," he added. "We all talked a lot, talked to the guys and said, 'Let's set a record.' We didn't have to fiddle with the car a lot. During the run, the lines were different on each lap. I was just trying to get more speed. I was able to run flat out. Today, I was really where I should have been yesterday with it but I wasn't able to because I had two engines let go.

"(Yesterday) there was a major vapor lock in the water system and after replacing it, it cooked the new engine in a matter of a lap."

Marco Greco, who had an engine failure on Pole Day, was next out and put the #41 AJ Foyt Enterprises machine into the field at a four-lap average of 228.840.

"It's great to (have) the fastest '94 car on the grid," Greco said. "My career has been very difficult in terms of people who want to give me a true opportunity. A.J. is the first one to give me what he said he would...no more, no less. This year, I don't feel like I'm alone. I hope from now on, I can have a good shot."

Luyendyk and Greco were the only qualifiers from the Sunday line. Aside from a one-lap run by Brad Murphey before an engine failure, no one pushed into line until late afternoon when Greco's teammate, Scott Sharp, went to the north end.

Sharp had also had a Pole Day engine failure and on his second attempt, he put together a smooth run of 231.201 at 3:13

With a bid for the pole denied, it was left for Arie Luyendyk to go for a track record that should stand for many years.

The 80th Indianapolis 500 would be the last for the current car specifications. In 1997, a new formula would be utilized by the Indy Racing League for a different type of car and slower speeds.

With his run disallowed on Saturday, Luyendyk made no secret of a quest for the records, practicing in the #5 Jonathan Byrd's Cafeteria/Bryant Heating & Cooling entry at 237.567 miles per hour in the morning session.

When the time came to qualify, Luyendyk reached his goal, putting together a solid four-lap run of 236.986 with a fastest lap of 237.498. He had lost the pole, but had bested Scott Brayton for the track records once again.

Luyendyk was the 23rd qualifier, and would start back in the field behind the first-day qualifiers.

"I've never gone through a roller coaster like this but we achieved one thing and that's breaking the track record," Luyendyk said. "Today's Mother's Day and yesterday was a

	Date:	Sunday, May 12
	Weather:	Cloudy, High 52°
Qualification Attempts:	7	
Qualifiers:	6	

| | Second Day Qualifiers | |
Car	Driver	Speed
5	Arie Luyendyk	236.986
11	Scott Sharp	231.201
41	Marco Greco	228.840
54	Robbie Buhl	226.217
96	Paul Durant	225.404
90	Racin Gardner	224.453

p.m. in the #11 Conseco AJ Foyt Racing entry.

"We thought we had a shot at one of the top two rows until the engine problems yesterday," Sharp said. "We went 233 this morning and definitely didn't want to limp into qualifying. We're going to plan on running to the front early, because if you wait very long, the leaders can get away from you. Maybe Arie and I should team up."

Paul Durant was next in the #96 ABF Motorsports USA Sunrise Rental Canada entry, a 1992 Lola Buick. The four-lap average for the west coast supermodified driver was 225.404.

"The car was still tight," Durant said. "It's

Scott Sharp

been tight since we got here. We made a couple of radical changes but they didn't make much of a difference. I couldn't take the line I wanted to, but I still feel pretty good. We're happy with where we're at."

It was left to "Happy Hour" for others to find speed, and both Robbie Buhl and Racin Gardner did before qualifications closed for the weekend.

Buhl put together a run of 226.217 in the #54 Original Coors/Beck Motorsports machine as the 27th qualifier of the month.

"We've been working on getting comfortable in the race car all day and my speed jump is a testament to my crew knowing what they were doing," Buhl said. "This car has never been raced before. This is the car that Al Unser tried to qualify in when he

Robbie Buhl

retired and Jeff Ward tried to qualify last year and didn't make it."

Gardner went out just three minutes before the track closed. He steered the #90 Team Scandia/Slick Gardner Enterprises entry to a four-lap average of 224.453.

"This morning we had a little bit of a push and were only going about 210," Gardner said. "But we worked with it and got it dialed in. Dick Simon has really helped me a lot this week. This is the first time I've been here and for the week, I've only run 80-89 laps. With all the rain, this is the first full day I've had to run."

Johnny O'Connell and Scott Harrington had passed the first two phases of their driver's tests and would use the second week to complete them and make their runs on the final weekend.

Twenty-seven cars were now in the field. Others continued the search for speed.

Right:
Marco Greco bounced back from a Pole Day engine failure to qualify at a speed of 228.840.

Johnny O'Connell

After a wild weekend of qualifications, those who had made the field prepared for Race Day and the others still sought speed.

And while this was going on, the yellow light flashed on three times for critters on the race track. Nobody could determine whether that was a track record or not, but one yellow was caused by a wayward chipmunk and the other two came about because of a persistent mother duck and nine ducklings who waddled into Turn 1...twice.

Amid all this, Michel Jourdain Jr. turned his fastest lap of the month at 234.223 miles per hour in the #22 Herdez Quaker State Canels entry. Tony Stewart was fastest of the day with a lap of 235.837 in the #20 Menards/Glidden/Quaker State Special.

Jourdain's lap was almost four miles per hour than his previous best. It spawned predictions of high speeds on Race Day.

Above: Spaniard Fermin Velez was still in search of enough speed to clinch his first Indy 500 starting bid.

"I think the weather helped," he said. "We weren't trying to go fast. It just happened. It's not windy. It was perfect. The car is set up for the race and after the fast lap, we did a full-tank run and the lap after (we started) was 229.

"We'd like to make some other runs," he added, "but if it's an emergency (such as extended rain), we're ready."

QUOTE OF THE DAY:
"They'll probably have to go through therapy." — Eliseo Salazar

As of this day, 16 drivers had exceeded 230 miles per hour in either practice or qualifications, three more than in 1995.

Johnny O'Connell and Tyce Carlson became the 15th and 16th driver's to pass the rookie test. Scott Harrington completed the third and fourth phases and Fermin Velez completed the second and third phases.

O'Connell was the quickest of drivers not yet in the field with a lap at 216.024 in the #75 Mechanics Laundry/Cunningham Racing entry, followed by Carlson at 210.393 in the #36 State Bail Bonding/Kelly's Pub Too machine.

Eliseo Salazar was second fastest of the day with a lap at 234.858 in the #7 Cristal/Copec/Mobil entry, despite being the driver most affected by the "critter yellows."

He was on the track when the ducks caused the first of their yellows, causing Speedway firemen to shoo them toward the Turn 1 creek.

"Actually, I was in the warmup lane when I saw them stopped in the grass," Salazar said. "Then, when I went into Turn 1 and saw them a couple of feet away, I had to swerve to miss them. I'm sure I scared them. They'll probably have to go through therapy for the rest of their lives."

Later, Salazar hit his second pigeon of the month.

"The bird was in the middle of Turn 1," Salazar said. "The car won the battle. But we missed the big family this morning."

Date:	Monday, May 13
Weather:	Cold, High 54°
Drivers On Track:	16
Cars On Track:	16
Total Laps:	488

Top Five Non-Qualified Drivers of the Day

Car	Driver	Speed
75	Johnny O'Connell	216.024
36	Tyce Carlson	210.393
39	Scott Harrington	203.804
43	Fermin Velez	201.676
15	Joe Gosek	198.522

QUOTE OF THE DAY:
"I had to wait my turn."
— Fermin Velez

Brad Murphey

Arie Luyendyk was the fastest, but Brad Murphey and Fermin Velez had the best reasons to be pleased on this day leading up to the final search for speed.

Luyendyk, already the official track record holder and comfortably in the field, turned a lap at 238.493 miles per hour in the #35 Jonathan Byrd's Cafeteria/Bryant Heating & cooling entry. It was the second-fastest practice lap in Speedway history.

Meanwhile, Murphey turned a lap at 228.612 in the #10 Hemelgarn Racing machine, fastest of the day among drivers not yet in the field.

Velez was second fastest of those ranks with a lap at 223.775 in the #43 Alta Spring Water/Perry Ellis/Royal Purple car after passing the fourth and observation phases of his driver's test.

"The Indy 500 will be the biggest accomplishment in my career," Velez said. "It's been a terrible 10 or 11 days because I had to wait my turn. When I got my turn, we started to find a bunch of little problems. So finally, we fixed everything and the car is running nicely."

Billy Boat made his first appearance on the track in the #87 Pagan Racing entry and passed the first phase of his driver's test. The car was the 1992 Lola used by Roberto Guerrero to set track records and take the pole in 1992.

Andy Michner also made his first appearance of the month, taking out the #36 State Bail Bonding/Kelly's Pub Too machine that had proven to be the "workhorse" for new drivers.

Off the track, Treadway Racing and McCormack Motorsports both announced that they would field cars built by G Force for 1997 Indy Racing League events. Treadway, which had announced it would use the Aurora engine earlier, became the first team to declare a car/engine combination under the League's new formula.

It was also announced that University of Colorado football coach Rick Neuheisel would serve on the pit crew of Buzz Calkins on Race Day.

"He'll either be on the deadman valve on the fuel tank or be the 'lollipop man' (holder of the stop sign to guide a driver to the pit)," Calkins said.

Meanwhile, Bruce Robertson, one of the Speedway's most dedicated fans, stopped by the press room. Robertson, who is blind from retinitis pigmentosa, and his guide dog Goldie have been regulars at the track for five years. Robertson said he can see cars immediately in front of him.

"I was here for Arie's fast lap — the 239 lap — and could tell he was going really fast," Bruce said. "I can tell by the sound how fast they are. I can also tell the difference between engines when they go by. I love the track. I like the engine noises and Goldie likes the people."

Right: Newcomer Billy Boat made his first appearance at the Speedway in a Pagan Racing entry.

	Date:	Tuesday, May 14
	Weather:	Rain, High 59°
	Drivers On Track:	17
	Cars On Track:	16
	Total Laps:	694

Top Five Drivers of the Day

Car	Driver	Speed
10	Brad Murphey	228.612
43	Fermin Velez	212.655
36	Dan Drinan	203.767
15	Joe Gosek	196.631
36	Andy Michner	193.690

The rain which had plagued practice throughout the month set its own new track records on this day.

Another complete washout boosted the total time lost to rain to 34 hours, 12 minutes of scheduled practice time. That broke the

A behind-the-wheel view of the cockpit demonstrates how differently a race car's dash reads than a passenger car.

mark of 25 hours, 37 minutes in 1973 — as far back as those kinds of records were reliable.

It also caused USAC Chief Steward Keith Ward to continue the sanctioning body's Rookie Orientation Program.

"We're going to start at 9 in the morning and if guys are ready, we'll try to get them finished up," Ward said.

QUOTE OF THE DAY:
"That's the way it should be."
— Larry Nash

That was welcome news to Billy Boat and Andy Michner. Boat had completed his first phase only and Michner was just getting started, with no laps completed toward his first phase.

Meanwhile, the atmosphere of cooperation among teams in Gasoline Alley continued.

The latest was an effort by Treadway Racing to help Scott Harrington and his LP Motorsports team.

"We're giving them a little setup information and our gearbox guy, Steve Eppard, is helping them out," said Buddy Lindblom, team manager for Treadway Racing. "Fred Treadway volunteered our help and we loaned them our old-style fuel nozzle and some rims that have been through inspection.

"The helping back and forth has gone on to a certain extent before. It actually helps both sides."

Larry Nash, team manager for Harrington's effort, welcomed the assistance.

"We've gotten bits and pieces for our race car from a few teams," Nash said. "We have an older car, a '92, so we've been able to acquire these parts from teams that ran these cars in the past.

"People have given us assistance here and there because we're a little low on the learning curve, so every bit helps."

Nash applauded the warm spirit that had developed in Gasoline Alley.

"It used to be this way and that's the way it should be," he said. "We've been away from this arena for awhile, so coming back now, it's like coming back home."

Date:	Wednesday, May 15
Weather:	Rain, High 61°
Drivers On Track:	0
Cars On Track:	0
Total Laps:	0

With two days remaining before the final weekend of time trials, this day provided some with hope and others with setbacks.

The hope came for Brad Murphey and Johnny O'Connell, who posted laps solidly in the 225 mile-per-hour range as the days wound down.

Murphey reached 225.875 miles per hour in the #10 Hemelgarn Racing entry and O'Connell turned a lap at 225.315 in the #75 Mechanics Laundry/Cunningham Racing machine.

Hope also came for Scott Harrington and Billy Boat, who became the 18th and 19th drivers to pass their driver's tests.

And it went away for Harrington, who slammed the Turn 3 wall at 1:28 p.m. in the #39 Harrington Motorsports/LP Racing entry, shortly after getting the "all clear" from the test.

Harrington escaped with a bruised left foot and left shoulder and was cleared to drive by Dr. Henry Bock, Speedway medical director. The car didn't fare as well, sustaining extensive damage from two impacts.

Rookie Justin Bell bowed out of the chase for the month of May, saying he would pass up the 1996 edition of the "500."

"This is how my week has been," Bell said. "It's like Michelle Pfeiffer knocking on your motel room door and saying, 'Oops, wrong room.'"

Boat eventually reached 224.657 miles per hour in the #99 Pagan Racing entry.

"Ten years ago when I was running Indy

Lights, I came here and the drama and excitement of this place was unbelievable," Boat said. "I knew this was what I wanted. But a year ago, I would never have had the chance. I'd be running a midget in California today."

Andy Michner completed three phases of his driver's test and Rob Wilson completed the first phase.

Arie Luyendyk continued to set the pace among qualified drivers with a lap at 234.540 in the #35 Jonathan Byrd's Cafeteria/Bryant Heating & Cooling entry.

Danny Ongais made his first appearance of the month, taking the track briefly in the #77 Brickell Racing entry.

Only one day of practice remained before the final spots in the field would be determined.

Above: Scott Harrington escaped with only bruises after his impact with the Turn #3 wall. Below: Johnny Unser's four-time Indy 500 winner Uncle Al (right) was on hand to provide some pointers.

Date:	Thursday, May 16
Weather:	Cloudy, High 71°
Drivers On Track:	23
Cars On Track:	22
Total Laps:	899

Top Five Non-Qualified Drivers of the Day

Car	Driver	Speed
10	Brad Murphey	225.875
75	Johnny O'Connell	225.315
99	Billy Boat	224.657
36	Dan Drinan	213.159
39	Scott Harrington	209.859

Above: John Menard mourned the loss of a great friend and race car driver, Scott Brayton (pictured below).

QUOTE OF THE DAY:
"Today we lost a great friend."
— *John Menard*

This day, which should have featured competition and the gains of speed for the final rounds of time trials will forever be known as one of the most tragic in Speedway history.

Scott Brayton, who had dramatically captured his second straight Indianapolis 500 pole, hit the wall in Turn 2 at 12:17 p.m. in the #23 Menards/Glidden/Quaker State Special after a right rear tire rapidly deflated.

Brayton, 37, died at 12:50 p.m. at Methodist Hospital. The Speedway delayed the announcement of Brayton's death until 4 p.m. so family members could be notified.

Later, Speedway President Tony George and Team menard owner John Menard met with the media in the Trackside Conference Room to talk about Brayton, the popular veteran.

"We're very saddened by Scott's death," George said. "He's been a great ambassador to our sport. His family has put their entire heart and soul into automobile racing. There's so much love in that family. They're so loved by the racing community. It is with a heavy heart that we sit before you today.

"Scott expressed to me earlier in the month on a couple of different occasions how much he loved his two girls — Becky and his daughter, Carly. We're going to miss Scott. He died doing what he loved, going fast at the Indianapolis Motor Speedway. There's not much more that can be said but that."

Menard expressed similar thoughts.

"Today we lost a great friend, a great husband, a great father and a great competitor," Menard said. "Words just can't describe how I feel right now. Scotty just loved this place. He loved running fast here, loved the competition. He was so proud of the fact he had the pole. He worked for that pole. It was a real gutsy thing he did Saturday (withdrawing a second-row car and going for the pole). He died doing what he loved.

"There are very, very heavy hearts at Team Menard right now. Scotty had a perfect race car, a perfect day and a perfect track and it reached out and bit him. It reminds you that this is a very serious business that we're about."

During the day, three other drivers passed rookie tests, raising the month's total to 22. Andy Michner, Joe Gosek and Rob Wilson completed the mission, but Michner said he wouldn't attempt to qualify.

Brad Murphey was the fastest of the day of drivers still bidding for a spot in the field with a lap at 228.548 miles per hour in the #10 Hemelgarn Racing entry. Billy Boat was next at 223.425 in the #99 Pagan Racing machine.

The third day of time trials would be next.

Date:	Friday, May 17
Weather:	Sunny, High 84°
Drivers On Track:	19
Cars On Track:	18
Total Laps:	643

Top Five Non-Qualified Drivers of the Day

Car	Driver	Speed
10	Brad Murphey	228.548
99	Billy Boat	223.425
43	Fermin Velez	217.802
36	Dan Drinan	214.997
75	Johnny O'Connell	214.117

As morning practice opened on the third day of time trials, five spots remained in the 33-car starting field. There were plenty of drivers trying to claim them.

One who would not get a chance to qualify was Dan Drinan, the USAC midget and Silver Crown driver who had worked hard all month to get up to speed.

At 9:35 a.m., Drinan hit the wall in the south short chute in a grinding crash in the #36 State Bail Bonding/Kelly's Pub Too machine that left him with left hip and foot fractures, a bruised left lung, a concussion and a trip to Methodist Hospital. He faced a long recovery period before rekindling his dream again.

Billy Boat was the fastest of the session in the #99 Pagan Racing entry with a lap at 224.165 miles per hour. As the first qualifier of the day at 11:04 a.m., Boat could muster only a four-lap average of 221.824 to become the 29th qualifier of the month.

Next up was Fermin Velez, who put the #34 Cristal/Copec Mobil machine in the field at a four-lap average of 222.487.

Brad Murphey, who had been in the 228 bracket solidly during the month but practiced in the morning at only 222.750, went to the line for his second attempt. He checked in with a four-lap average of 226.053 in the #10 Hemelgarn Racing entry.

Johnny Parsons was next to go, in the #16 Team Blueprint Racing machine that had been repaired from a crash earlier in the month. He registered a four-lap run of 223.843 to gain his first berth in a "500" field in 10 years.

After that, others waited. Danny Ongais, officially assigned to the #77 Brickell Racing Group entry, breezed through his 20-lap refresher test.

With just one minute remaining in the day, Johnny O'Connell staged the final qualifying run in the #75 Mechanics Laundry/Cunningham Racing machine. He became

QUOTE OF THE DAY:
"We've been chasing gremlins all day."
— Johnny O'Connell

the 33rd qualifier of the month at a four-lap average of 222.361, locked safely in the field.

"With all the boost problems we were having, when we did 225 the other day, it's been downhill the rest of the way," O'Connell said. "We've been chasing gremlins all day. This place is awfully important. If we had to wait another year, we would've waited. I have a lot to learn. I was happy to be the last one out. I can see why they call it 'Happy Hour.' It makes you happy. What an emotional rollercoaster...the highs and lows of this place."

After the track closed, a memorial service was held for Scott Brayton in the Victory Lane area of the Tower Terrace. A huge crowd of team members, officials and fans turned out to pay their respects.

One day remained before the field would be set for the 80th running of the Indianapolis 500.

Johnny Parsons qualified for his 12th Indy 500 starting field in 27th spot.

Date:	Saturday, May 18
Weather:	Sunny, High 85°
Qualification Attempts:	5
Qualifiers:	5

Third Day Qualifiers

Car	Driver	Speed
10	Brad Murphey	226.438
16	Johnny Parsons	223.843
34	Fermin Velez	222.487
75	Johnny O'Connell	222.361
99	Billy Boat	221.824

Scott Harrington

The finishing touches on the starting field for the Indianapolis 500 started even before qualifying on this final day of time trials.

Team Menard representatives announced that Danny Ongais had been assigned to the #2 Glidden Menards Special qualified by the late Scott Brayton.

"It was an emotional day yesterday," said Larry Curry, the team's director of racing. "Scott worked so hard to put this car in the race. When Danny ran on a fulltime basis, Danny ran fast. Scott lived to go fast. I think it's fitting for Danny to be in Scott's car on Race Day and it's a great tribute to Scott."

On the track, Hideshi Matsuda made his first appearance of the month, and quickly

Below: Rookie Randy Tolsma's hopes for a spot in the starting field were dashed when he collided with the south short chute wall.

	Date:	Sunday, May 19
	Weather:	Cloudy, High 80°
Qualification Attempts:		5
	Qualifiers:	3

Fourth Day Qualifiers

Car	Driver	Speed
52	Hideshi Matsuda	226.746
44	Scott Harrington	225.135
43	Joe Gosek	222.793

(Bumps #99 Billy Boat)

QUOTE OF THE DAY:
"I'd walk before I'd give up a chance."
— *Scott Harrington*

reached a top practice lap of 227.147 miles per hour by early afternoon in the #52 Beck Motorsports entry.

Matsuda had made a practice of jumping into a car and going fast in each of the previous two years and could be counted on for a quality run.

Tyce Carlson got into the #77 Brickell Racing Group entry, replacing Ongais.

At 1:50 p.m., Randy Tolsma's hopes were dashed when hit the outside wall in the south short chute in the #24 McCormack Motorsports entry. The car had right-side damage. Tolsma was examined and released from Hanna Medical Center.

Matsuda went to the line at 4:02 p.m. and reeled off a four-lap average of 226.856 miles per hour. He had had only 35 laps of practice.

"When I went back to Japan last year, I thought every night how to run this race and maybe that's the secret for today," Matsuda said.

With Matsuda's qualifying run, Billy Boat was getting close to the "bubble." Hedging against that eventuality, he took out the #84 AJ Foyt Enterprises entry as a possible backup. But at 5:24 p.m., his month of May ended when he hit the wall in the south short chute. The car was extensively damaged and Boat was transported to Methodist Hospital with back and leg pain.

A few minutes later, Scott Harrington and the #44 Della Penna Motorsports Ralph's Food 4 Less Fuji Film entry were pushed into the qualifying line.

After Harrington's earlier accident which wiped out LP Racing's only car, an arrangement was made with John Della Penna for Harrington to take over the backup to Richie Hearn.

He had one shot to make the field and qualified at a four-lap average of 222.185. That filled the field and put Boat, now in the hospital, on the "bubble" with just 23 minutes remaining.

"We had problems with the car (and) we were over one week late in getting here to the track," Harrington said. "I had just completed my rookie test when the car was destroyed. A lot of people stepped up and helped us out when that happened and fortunately we came up with some sponsorship money. We even had fans coming up and giving us money."

Harrington had sold his Porsche to get the opportunity to come to the Speedway.

"If I had a choice between running Indy or driving a nice car, I'd walk before I'd give up a chance to run here," Harrington said.

At 5:42 p.m., Joe Gosek, who had switched from the Tempero-Giuffre team to Team Scandia, took out the #43 Alta Spring Water/Perry Ellis/Royal Purple entry. He became the 36th qualifier of the month with a run of 222.793, bumping Boat from the field and putting Harrington on the "bubble."

Tyce Carlson, in the #77 Brickell Racing Earl's Performance PDM entry was the last to have a shot. He waved off after one lap at 218.441. The team pushed back into line quickly, and with three minutes remaining, Carlson took a final shot. His run of 221.201 was too slow, the gun went off and the field was set.

Even though he missed the show, Carlson

was pleased to get a last-ditch shot at the field.

"I'm just grateful that we got an opportunity," Carlson said. "At 11 this morning, I didn't even have a ride. At 11, they told me to go get my driver's suit, so I had to break into my buddy's car just to get it. But I figured there was no way I was going to miss this just because I couldn't get my suit.

"I really want to be a part of the IRL. Living in Indianapolis and growing up here...this is where I belong."

So the field was set, with all the drama of years past. It was on to Race Day.

Above: Joe Gosek bumped his way into the field, moving Billy Boat to first alternate. Left: Armed Forces Day at the Speedway included a full color guard. Below: Team Menard announced that Danny Ongais would drive the #32 car on Race Day.

47

Above: Team Galles won the Coors Pit Stop Challenge for the fourth time, this year with driver Davy Jones. Below: Roberto Guerrero and Pagan Racing finished second in the pit stop contest.

Carburetion Day...the final session of practice had arrived. After this session, the track would be closed until Race Day, when the drama of the 80th running of the "500" would be the finale to the efforts of all who had labored tirelessly during the month of May.

Rain caused a yellow after 23 minutes of green time, but it wasn't early enough to help Johnny Unser.

At 1:32 p.m., Unser did a half-spin in Turn 4 and hit both the outside and inside walls in the #64 Ruger Titanium/Project Indy/Reynard machine. Unser had a bruised left foot and was released to drive.

The car sustained left front suspension, nose-cone and front wing damage and a bent right rear wheel and the Project Indy crew would have additional work to do before Race Day.

Shortly thereafter, the rains hit and teams waited throughout the day to get a few more precious moments of practice. That came at 5:51 p.m. and with three additional minor caution periods, the track closed at 6:15 p.m.

Tony Stewart was the fastest of the day at 231.273 miles per hour in the #20 Menards/Glidden/Quaker State Special. Team Menard teammate Eddie Cheever was next at 230.621 in the #3 Quaker State Menards Special, followed by Buddy Lazier at 230.598 in the #91 Hemelgarn Racing-Delta Faucet-Montana entry and Eliseo Salazar at 230.208 in the #7 Cristal/Copec Mobil machine.

Danny Ongais was the fastest of the final short session with a lap at 226.364 in the #32 Glidden Menards Special. It was his first time in the car as the replacement for the late Scott Brayton.

All but three eligible cars participated in the practice. Those which didn't were the #16 of Johnny Parsons, which had a transmission problem; the #99 of Billy Boat, who was not medically cleared to drive and the #77 of Tyce Carlson, the second alternate.

The Coors Pit Stop Challenge was held and Team Galles, with chief mechanic Mitch Davis and driver Davy Jones, bested the #99

Date:	Thursday, May 23
Weather:	Rain, High 64°
Drivers On Track:	32
Cars On Track:	32
Total Laps:	633

Top Five Drivers of the Day

Car	Driver	Speed
20	Tony Stewart	231.273
3	Eddie Cheever	230.621
91	Buddy Lazier	230.598
7	Eliseo Salazar	230.208
5	Arie Luyendyk	228.380

Pagan Racing crew in the final. Team Galles posted a time of 14.176 seconds to the Pagan team's 16.368. It marked the fourth time that Team Galles had won the contest.

Meanwhile, others reflected on the month as only the biggest day of the month was before them.

"I think what has happened this month, when everyone was thinking the rookies will wreak havoc, has not happened," said Buzz Calkins. "This month, the rookies have shown just the opposite."

"Today, it was neat to be able to walk down pit lane

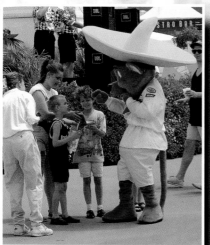

with all the people calling your name," said Richie Hearn. "They were there, even though they knew it was going to rain."

"It is a different year with the other guys in Michigan," said Arie Luyendyk. "We have a lot of quality people from sprints, midgets and other forms of racing...just not a lot of Indy experience. We talked to the rookies...maybe too much."

"One thing we have in common is that racing is our lives," said Michel Jourdain Jr. "It doesn't matter where you come from. You all want to win. We are rookies, but we all want to have a safe race and all want to finish the race. This was the biggest dream of my life. I came here in 1991 to watch my uncle (Bernard) and hoped I could be here, but I didn't think it would be so soon."

"It could be a problem with 33 veterans, too," said Roberto Guerrero. "There's huge pressure on all of us. Something can happen with anybody, really. I think everyone will take extra care of each other and have a safe race."

And Eliseo Salazar was asked what the Team Scandia veterans told the team's rookies.

"We told them not to beat us," Salazar replied. "We're the veterans."

Above: Eliseo Salazar was fourth fastest in the final practice with a top speed of 230.208. Left: Speedy Gonzales entertained visitors to the second annual Indy FanFest. Below: Hundreds of Viper owners arrived to cruise the most famous 2.5 miles in the world.

500 Festival

Indianapolis Life 500 Festival Mini-Marathon

SETTING A FRIENDLY PACE

500 Festival Queen Jamie Danielle Norris and 500 Festival President Ramon Humke

Bank One 500 Festival Rookie Run Winners

BEFORE THE ROAR

The very
popular Jim
Nabors prepares
to sing "Back
Home Again In
Indiana."

Miss
Florence
Henderson
delivers the
National
Anthem.

Shortly
before giving the
command, "Lady and
Gentlemen, Start Your
Engines," Chairman of the
Board Emeritus Mary Fendrich
Hulman is visited by four-time
500 winner A.J.Foyt, a longtime
friend of the family.

53

mitment to Run

By Mark Robinson

As the adage goes, you have to walk before you can run.

That does not mean you must be able to walk before you can race. Buddy Lazier's winning effort in the 1996 Indianapolis 500 is a shining example.

Barely able to walk due to numerous fractures in his backbone, Lazier ambled gingerly to his race car that overcast May morning for the start of the 80th spectacle. Yet, once strapped into the cockpit of his rocket, the courageous Coloradoan displayed all the ability necessary to capture auto racing's most storied event. And it was no Sunday drive through the park.

Lazier was a contender all day in his Hemelgarn Racing Reynard with Ford-Cosworth power, dodging the potential pitfalls from 10 caution periods to keep the leaders in sight. He saved his most daring driving for when it counted. Charging at breakneck speed, Lazier moved from third to first in the final 10 laps and held off runner-up Davy Jones by 0.695 of a second at the checkered flag.

The third-closest finish in Indy 500 history capped an exciting, action-filled day that left more than the winning team smiling. Indianapolis Motor Speedway president Tony George was beaming after the first 500 run under the Indy Racing League banner came off with nary a hitch, and was as competitive and entertaining as any of the previous 79.

The fact that a talented and deserving American driver like the 29-year-old Lazier wound up on the victory platform was the coup-de-grace.

That Lazier was able to compete at Indianapolis at all, much less win, was no small feat. The amiable driver suffered 16 fractures and numerous bone chips in his back in a serious practice crash at Phoenix just two months before coming to Indy. For a while, Lazier wasn't certain he'd be healed enough to drive at the Brickyard.

"I was in a hospital bed for three weeks," Lazier said of his recovery. "A month ago, I was barely able to walk. For a while, I had given up a lot of hope for this event.

"I thought it was going to take everything I had plus some to get here," he added. "When you have a family that supports you like mine does, it makes all the difference in the world. We made the commitment to run here. Period. Whatever it took."

It took a concerted effort on the part of the entire Ron Hemelgarn team the entire month. The pain and discomfort limited how many hot laps Lazier could drive in practice. A specially designed seat by Dr. Brock Walker helped, but "I literally spent the whole month in a lot of pain," Lazier admitted.

Somehow, Lazier was able to maintain his concentration and fight off the pain for 200 laps and nearly 3 1/2 hours in the race, which started just 15 minutes late despite early-

Opposite: Wet weather greeted fans on race morning, yet the rains held off to start the 80th Indianapolis 500 on schedule.

15
16
17
18
19
20
21
22
23
24
25
26
27
28
29
30
31
32
33

Hideshi Matsuda's
car (inset) failed to
start at the signal
and was pushed to
the south pits,
where it was fired
just in time to join
the field for the
green.

morning rains that drenched the track.

The Speedway president himself pitched in on the clean-up effort by donating the sweater off his back to help dry water that had dripped from the flag stand onto the yard of brick at the start-finish line.

"I didn't get down to the head of the field as I normally do to see my grandmother (Mary Fendrich Hulman) give the command to start the race," George said. "I was still at the start-finish line with the leak, where I donated my sweater to the cause."

When the green flag fell, Tony Stewart, who inherited the pole position when Menard teammate Scott Brayton was killed in a practice crash May 17, bolted into the lead ahead of fellow front-row starters Eliseo Salazar and Jones. The safe, clean start of all 33 drivers including 17 rookies, served to quiet critics who thought the green field might struggle in the massive wind tunnel known as the start of the Indianapolis 500. In light of the parade lap melee that ensued later in the day at Michigan International Speedway, the critics all but disappeared.

Stewart, the sensational rookie from nearby Rushville, Ind., would dominate the first quarter of the race in his Lola with stock-block Menard power. Stewart led the initial 31 laps and 44 of the first 54 before his engine began to sour. Sidelined in 24th place after 82 laps, Stewart initially fired blame at his USAC-specified pop-off valve, the last time that excuse can be used at Indy since 1997 plans call for a switch to normally aspirated engines, making the popoff valve obsolete.

"I was running down on boost," Stewart reported, "trying to conserve fuel, and (the valve) blew in my ear, so I turned (the boost)

down some more and it blew in my ear again, and it blew a third time.

"Every time that valve pops off it hurts the engine. The third time did it."

Mike Devin, USAC's director of operations, disputed Stewart's assertion, saying Team Menard's own engine builder told him Stewart burned an engine valve that had no relation to the pop-off valve.

Regardless, Stewart became the third Indy rookie to lead in his first lap of competition, and his 44 laps led were third most of the day and the most by a rookie since Bill Holland paced 143 in 1947. Stewart also set the all-time race record for fastest lap by the race leader when, on lap 10, he was clocked at 234.421 miles an hour.

With Stewart's demise, the battle for the lead settled on a swift but select few drivers. Jones, Lazier and Roberto Guerrero all took turns at the front, but each certainly had an eye in the mirror for the blazing No. 5 car of Arie Luyendyk.

Luyendyk, the 1990 "500" winner, was the record-setting fast qualifier in 96 but started 20th after his pole-day qualifying run was disallowed because his car was underweight. Despite his seventh-row start, the Flying Dutchman was the widely-held race favorite because of his experience and the Reynard/Ford/Firestone package he was piloting.

Early returns proved the prognosticators had the right idea. Luyendyk was clearly the class of the field. By lap 10, he had motored up 12 spots to eighth. By lap 40 he was fifth despite brushing the wall on lap 24. Twenty circuits later he was third. At lap 90, only Lazier separated Luyendyk from the lead.

Luyendyk was still running second when

Rookie phenom Tony Stewart led 44 laps before falling out with engine problems.

he pitted on lap 97 under the caution period caused when Brad Murphey's car brushed the wall in Turn 2. Despite stalling his car, Luyendyk was still in good stead as he exited his pit at the head of pit row. But, as he maintained his line on the inside of the pit exit lane, Luyendyk's car was sideswiped by that of Salazar, whose left wheels did significant damage to the right side of Luyendyk's machine.

Luyendyk limped back around to the pits, where a 10-minute stop was required for repairs. He

returned to the race but logged only 149 laps before his day ended in 16th place.

"I thought I was in my lane," said a bewildered Luyendyk, obviously sensing a chance at a second Indy victory snatched away for no sound reason. "I thought I was where I was supposed to be.

"Unfortunately, I stalled it in the pits and I guess the consequence of that was the crash leaving the pits.

"So maybe I should blame myself."

Salazar's Lola sustained minimal damage, so he remained in contention just enough to wreak havoc on another potential winner later in the race.

First, though, the victory chances for Guerrero, a two-time Indy runner-up, were dashed. The native Colombian and naturalized American led more laps (47) than any

driver in the 96 race, including 25 consecutive from laps 134-158. He was still solidly in contention when he came to the pits for a splash of fuel under yellow on lap 167.

But a seal on the fuel hose nozzle failed and Guerrero was the one splashed with methanol.

"The car never actually caught fire but I got bathed in fuel and one of our (crewmen) was trying to get me out, and I didn't want to get out," Guerrero said. "No way."

In his struggle to maintain his seat in the cockpit, Guerrero dislodged his two-way radio plug and was unable to communicate with his crew the rest of the race. By the time things were cleared and Guerrero left his pit, 1 minute, 42 seconds had elapsed. He was a lap down and out of the victory picture.

When the green flag re-emerged on lap 169, Jones was the leader and trailed only Salazar in the line behind the pace car. Opting to get past Salazar and run in clean air, Jones ducked to the inside of the frontstretch as the course went green. But Salazar wouldn't let Jones Lola-Mercedes- Benz get by.

Twice, Salazar intentionally pulled his car to the inside to block Jones pass attempt. The second time it forced Jones to graze the retaining wall to the pit road. Jones had to back off the accelerator to avoid Salazar and a potential catastrophic accident at the head of the field.

Jones surrendered the lead to Alessandro Zampedri. What's more, he also surrendered some of the delicate balance in his car.

"He was a lap down and I didn't really need to get by him," Jones said of Salazar. "But I wanted to get out in some clean air and pull some distance away from second place.

"I don't know what he was thinking," Jones added, his emotion increasing by the word. "You don't need to use some sort of blocking tactics and stuff people into the wall, but he did coming down the front straightaway. We worked so hard during the race to get the balance right but it knocked the front of the car out a little bit, where I had too much push at the end."

Despite the balance of Jones Lola being slightly askew, he was able to remain on Zampedri's tail, and he actually chased down and overtook the Italian on lap 190, 10 circuits shy of the finish.

But Lazier was charging as well, saving his best laps for the trophy dash to the checkers. "The car was really good as the fuel ran down," Lazier said, "which was to our advantage."

Indeed. Lazier blew by Zampedri for second place on the back straight on lap 191. Just a tour later, he moved to the outside and passed Jones shortly after he crossed the start-finish line to begin lap 193.

Lazier proceeded to post his three fastest laps of the race 230.4 mph on lap 193, 232.9 on 194 and 229.8 on 195 to pull away.

The only thing Lazier didn't need and what Jones was pining for was another caution. It happened on lap 196, when Scott

the mishap, none was on the same lap. Guerrero thought he was passing for position, not realizing he was a lap behind Zampedri and a lap ahead of Salazar. Had his radio not been rendered inoperable by the pit incident on lap 167, Guerrero may have been aware a pass was not necessary.

"I could have put it in third gear and it wouldn't have mattered," he said regretfully.

Following Lazier and Jones across the fin-

Above: Roberto Guerrero and crew stayed at the front of the field for more than 117 miles, leading the most race laps. Right: Another veteran, Eddie Cheever, posted the fastest race lap at 236.103 mph, a new track record.

Sharp, running a strong fifth, found some oil in Turn 2 and hit the wall. The Speedway track crew made quick work of the clean-up, however, in time for the green flag to return on the 200th and final lap.

Only back marker Michel Jourdain Jr. was between Lazier and Jones as they sped toward Turn 1 for the final time, but it was enough. By the time Jones disposed of Jourdain in the backstretch, Lazier had opened an insurmountable cushion. Buddy embraced Duane Sweeney's checkered flag to signal the winner of the 80th running of the spectacle.

At the instant the checkered was waving for Lazier, a serious incident was taking place in Turn 4. Guerrero lost control of his Reynard-Ford and it collected the Lola-Fords of Zampedri and Salazar on its way to the outside wall.

Zampedri's car was sent airborne and then upside down along the frontstretch. The force of the collision with the wall and retaining fence sheared the nose off his car, exposing Zampedri's legs to serious injury. He suffered numerous fractures to his legs and feet, eventually losing a portion of his left foot to amputation.

Sadly, it was an accident that could have been avoided. For awhile the drivers held the fourth through sixth positions at the time of

ish line, and the only other driver to complete all 200 laps, was Richie Hearn. The third-place effort landed Hearn the Bank One "Rookie-of-the-Year" award.

Despite the last-lap crash, Zampedri finished fourth, Guerrero fifth and Salazar sixth. Danny Ongais, the oldest driver in the race after he was named to replace the late Scott Brayton in the Team Menard Lola-Menard, drove an admirable race to finish seventh.

Ongais was the top finisher of the four Menard entries despite the least seat time. While the other three drivers, Stewart, Eddie Cheever and Mark Dismore, were posting record speeds during the race, Ongais plodded along to finish three laps off the pace.

Cheever, who had engine problems and wound up 11th, was the most swift of the high-horsepower Menard machines. He had nine of the 11 fastest individual laps of the race, including a blistering 236.103 journey on lap 78. That was nearly seven mph better than the previous race record of 229.118 held by Michael Andretti in 92. That standard was so obsolete in 96 that at least 50 race laps were turned at a greater speed.

Sharp, who finished 10th despite his own accident, and 17th-place finisher Buzz Calkins tied for the initial IRL season championship, which consisted of three races.

But the spotlight was cast on Lazier; and deservedly so. Not only did he become the 11th driver to gain his first championship car victory at Indianapolis, he gave longtime owner/sponsor Hemelgarn his first victory and Firestone tires its first win at Indy since 1971.

"For seven or eight years, I've worked the pits, looking for a ride, pulling together local sponsors, just to try to get some equipment to show that you have the ability, who came to Indianapolis for the first time in 1989 but had been in only three "500s" before his winning entry. That makes this extra sweet. It all makes this extra sweet."

And it was in no way tainted in Lazier's mind because some name drivers opted not to race at Indy.

"It is the Indianapolis 500," he asserted. "As many years as I've raced and been around here, this field would have equaled any other field in the past. I'd love to be out here with everybody, but at the same time there's some great drivers here.

"And judging by the way the whole race went showed there's some real ability and some talent. Take a look at the speeds. Take a look at the start of the race."

Hemelgarn, Lazier's car owner, agreed.

"This is the greatest race in the world and always will be," the affable owner said.

It proved to be quite a turnaround in emotions for Hemelgarn in one year's time. In the 1995 race, one of his longtime drivers, Stan Fox, was critically injured in an opening-lap crash. Nearly fully recovered, Fox watched Lazier's triumph from the Hemelgarn pit.

"The greatest thrill I experienced was when Buddy took the checkered flag and I turned around to see Stan smiling his crooked smile, when just 365 days before that we didn't know if he would live. I've experienced the thrill of victory twice and Stan has

experienced the thrill of life.

"It was very hard last year when Stan was fighting for his life," Hemelgarn added. "It was the hardest Indy 500 I've been through. And to see Stan with his smile was a big victory. The Indy 500 is the greatest race in the world. My sights were set here in 1964 when I was looking through the fence while standing on a trash can. I worked very hard to get here. I think the Good Lord rewards you for things well done."

In the eyes of IMS president Tony George, it was a rewarding experience all the way around. The thrilling race punctuated a memorable inaugural Indy Racing League campaign.

"Everybody here did a great job," George said, "from the track crews to the teams to the drivers and the race officials. I think critics will always be critics, but we will just continue to try to prove that we have a product and an idea that wants development, and we will continue to develop it the best we can.

"Hopefully, in two to three years, people will realize that it is a quality series and a quality championship. Buddy Lazier is an excellent representation of the type of opportunity we are trying to create."

Team owner Ron Hemelgarn and the newest Indy 500 winner Buddy Lazier shared the thrill of winning the World's Greatest Race.

By Bruce Martin

MONTH OF SPEED

earlier. After the first day of qualifications were completed, Luyendyk's original four-lap average of 233.390 mph was disallowed when his car did not pass a post-qualification technical inspection because it was seven pounds too light.

This is the final season for the 2.6-liter, turbocharged engine formula at the Indianapolis 500 as the Indy Racing League switches to a 4.0-liter, normally-aspirated, production-based engine

The 80th Indianapolis 500 featured a "Month of Speed" unlike any other in the long-history of the Indianapolis Motor Speedway.

Arie Luyendyk firmly etched his name into the Indianapolis 500 record book when he won the 1990 Indy 500 at an average speed of 185.981 miles an hour.

He firmly established himself as the "King of Speed" at the Indianapolis Motor Speedway. During his qualification attempt on May 12, Luyendyk recorded the fastest single lap in IMS history at 237.498 miles an hour. His four-lap average was a Speedway record 236.986 mph. making him the fastest driver in the field for the Indianapolis 500.

These records helped redeem Luyendyk, who was knocked off the pole by the late Scott Brayton one day

beginning at the Indy 200 at Walt Disney World on Jan. 25, 1997. The new engine rules, combined with change to the cars, are expected to decrease the speeds by over 20 mph at Indianapolis.

The "Month of Speed" featured the fastest rookie in Indianapolis 500 history in Tony Stewart. It featured the fastest 33-car field ever. And it featured the fastest race lap in history when **Eddie Cheever**

turned a lap at 236.103 miles an hour on the 78th lap of the race in a Lola/Menard V6 for Team Menard.

Tony Stewart was fast all month. In fact, he topped the speed charts on the very first day the track was open for practice. Because of the large number of rookies in this year's Indianapolis 500, IRL and Speedway officials decided to devote the first few days of practice to the Rookie Orientation Program.

It didn't take long for Stewart to get up to speed. The first man ever to win three major national championships in one season when Stewart won the United States Auto Club (USAC) Midget, Sprint and Silver Crown series in 1995, showed why he is considered a star of the future.

On Monday, May 6, Stewart reached 231.774 miles an hour just 19 minutes after the track had opened. At that time, it was the fastest practice lap for a rookie in the history of the Indianapolis Motor Speedway.

Later in the day, Stewart shattered all speed records at IMS with a lap at 237.336 mph.

When the veterans were allowed to take the track on Tuesday, May 7, speeds continued to escalate. On Thursday, May 9, Luyendyk established himself as a speed demon when he ran a lap at 237.774 mph, at that time the fastest lap ever at the Indianapolis Motor Speedway. Stewart kept pace with a lap at 237.029 mph.

Luyendyk flirted with the once unthinkable mark of 240 miles an hour on Friday, May 10. Under dark, threatening skies Luyendyk ran a lap that is likely to stand the test of time at the Indianapolis Motor Speedway at 239.260 mph.

What was left for Luyendyk on Pole Day was a chance at starting first in the Indianapolis 500, and placing his name in the record book with the official fastest lap in Speedway history. Only laps run in the race and qualifications count as official Indianapolis Motor Speedway records.

But Pole Day would not turn out the way Luyendyk had hoped. After rain delayed the final practice session prior to pole qualifications by nearly four hours, Luyendyk barely missed a wheel that had flown off Johnny Parsons' car when it crashed into the third turn wall. Later in the same practice session, Luyendyk's car suffered an engine problem, which forced the team to prepare another car for the driver. The second car was the same car Luyendyk drove on his 239.260 mile an hour lap the previous day.

It would be tough for any other race in the world to match the drama that was evident at the Indianapolis Motor Speedway during the first weekend of qualifications.

When **Scott Brayton** made one of the biggest gambles in Indianapolis Motor history to win the pole for the 80th Indianapolis 500, there was never any doubt in his mind that it wasn't going to pay off.

Brayton had earlier qualified for the sixth starting position with a four-lap average of 231.535 mph. But he decided to switch to his backup car and withdraw the speed for the original car.

With just 18 minutes left in the qualification session, Brayton knocked Luyendyk off the pole when he established a record four-lap record of 233.718 mph. That allowed Brayton to win the Indianapolis 500 pole for the second year in a row.

Luyendyk had earlier knocked Brayton's teammate, Tony Stewart, off the pole. But Luyendyk's speed of 233.390 mph was later disallowed after his car was seven pounds under the minimum weight of 1,550 pounds in the post-qualifying technical inspection. The car was not disqualified, but the speed was disallowed, which meant Luyendyk had to make another qualification attempt the next day.

Despite the Luyendyk infraction, it didn't demean the huge gamble Brayton and his Team Menard operation made by pulling an already qualified car out of the Indianapolis 500 starting lineup.

"I knew we had to do it," said Brayton's team owner, John Menard. "We have been working on it all afternoon. It was a little high-stakes poker we were playing, but it paid off. I think this pole is better than last year because for Scott to do it two years in a row, man, this is great."

Brayton responded to the challenge

and became the first back-to-back pole winner at the Indianapolis 500 since Rick Mears in 1988-89.

"Nothing is more exciting than the Indianapolis Motor Speedway on Pole Day," Brayton said. "The Indianapolis 500 is what Indy car racing is all about.

"You can't take that away from the people because there are a lot of people who love this place."

Unfortunately for Luyendyk, his second starting position was taken from him after his car failed the post-qualifying technical inspection.

It didn't take long for Luyendyk to achieve redemption. One day after he was knocked out of the front row, Luyendyk switched to another car and shattered both the one-lap and four-lap qualification records at the Indianapolis Motor Speedway.

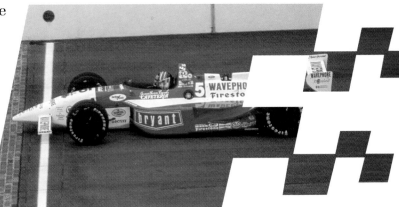

Luyendyk ran his 1995 Reynard/Ford-Cosworth to a four-lap average of 236.986 miles an hour on Sunday, May 11. On the final lap of his run, Luyendyk established the one-lap record of 237.498 mph. In fact, all four of his laps during his qualification attempts were Speedway records.

But he would not start on the pole because his qualification run came on the second day. Because of that, Brayton retained the pole from his run on Saturday, May 10. The last time the pole winner did not have the fastest speed in the Indianapolis 500 was in 1991, when Rick Mears won the pole with a four-lap run of 224.113 mph but Gary Bettenhausen went 224.468 the next day.

At 12:10 p.m. EST on May 11, Luyendyk started his qualification attempt and

drove
into
history.

"As long as we got the record today, that was our goal," Luyendyk said. "At least we achieved one of those goals this weekend. To have the record is an honor for sure because the Indianapolis Motor Speedway has so much history. To be part of that history is neat because in your career, you set goals."

Despite Luyendyk's record speed, he would have to start behind all the first day qualifiers, which put him in the 21st starting position - the outside of row seven. Unfortunately, sometimes speed comes with a price. And Scott Brayton paid the ultimate price when the pole winner was killed in a crash during practice at the Speedway on Friday, May 17.

Brayton knew the gambles that were involved in the high-speed, high stakes game of auto racing.

"It is the Indianapolis Motor Speedway and it is the most unpredictable game that you ever tried to play," Brayton said on May 4. "Trust me, this place does not play favorites, but it tends to reward those who persevere and lots of times acknowledges people who don't get that type of acknowledgment anywhere else.

"You have to put it in perspective, this is Las Vegas in its finest hour. It is big-time excitement and gambling all rolled into one event. If you control the dice, there would be no Las Vegas. If you could control a race car for every element, there wouldn't be an Indianapolis 500."

Brayton's death was the first time in history the pole winner of the Indianapolis 500 had been killed before the race.

He would be replaced in the car by Danny Ongais, a veteran of 10 Indianapolis 500s who last raced at the Speedway in 1986. **Tony Stewart** was moved from the middle of the front row to the pole position, which left the young rookie with the tremendous responsibility of leading the 33-car starting field to the green flag to start the race. The 33-car field average of 227.807 miles an hour was the fastest in the history of the race.

Stewart led 44 of the first 54 laps before dropping out of the race with engine failure on the 81st lap. Stewart recorded the fastest leading lap in Indy 500 history when he led the 10th lap at 234.412 miles an hour.

Further back in the field, Arie Luyendyk had moved from 20th starting position to second place by the 90th lap. But Luyendyk's bid at victory ended on the 98th lap when he was involved in a collision with Eliseo Salazar as both cars were entering the pit warmup lane following their pit stops.

By the end of the race, **Buddy Lazier** became the master of speed when it mattered most by passing Davy Jones at the start/finish line for the lead just eight laps from the checkered flag. Lazier won a dramatic Indianapolis 500 and placed his name among some of the all-time great champions in the history of "The World's Greatest Race."

Bruce Martin is the auto racing editor for United Press International and covers Indy car racing for National Speed Sport News.

BUDDY
LAZIER

#91 Hemelgarn Racing-Delta Faucet-Montana
Entrant: Hemelgarn Racing, Inc.   Crew Chief: Brian Nott

Buddy Lazier was the fastest in pre-season testing at both Walt Disney World and Phoenix and wound up with the first track record at Walt Disney World Speedway and the pole position for the inaugural Indy 200. He led 28 laps of the race before brake problems sidelined him.

It was in Phoenix where he suffered the most serious setback of his career. During practice, he spun in Turn 2 and collected Lyn St. James. Lazier's car briefly became airborne before slamming the wall backwards, breaking his back in several places.

Still recovering when May began, he ran a limited practice schedule but still reached 231.161 miles per hour on Day 6 and 234.381 on Day 7. Lazier was the second qualifier on Pole Day and checked in with a four-lap average of 231.468, starting fifth.

On Race Day, Lazier and the Hemelgarn team stayed to their plan. He stayed close to the front early and eventually led five times for 43 laps. He got his final lead by passing Davy Jones on Lap 193 and held Jones back on a last-lap restart to capture the 80th running of the Indianapolis 500.

"It was extremely, extremely sweet coming off the injury," Lazier said. "A month ago, I was barely able to walk. For awhile, I had given up a lot of hope for this event. It hasn't sunk in yet. It's probably gonna take some time. It's just awesome. The trophy? Awesome. The paycheck? Really awesome."

1996 INDY 500 PERFORMANCE PROFILE

Starting Position:	5
Qualifying Average:	231.468 MPH
Qualifying Speed Rank:	7
Best Practice Speed:	234.381 MPH 5/10
Total Practice Laps:	125
Number Practice Days:	6
Finishing Position:	1
Laps Completed:	200 147.956 MPH
Highest Position 1996 Race:	1
Fastest Race Lap:	194 232.907 MPH
1996 INDY 500 Prize Money:	$ 1,367,854
INDY 500 Career Earnings:	$ 1,840,730
Career INDY 500 Starts:	3
Career Best Finish:	1st 1996

1996 IRL PERFORMANCE PROFILE

IRL Points Championship:	11th, 159 points
IRL Best Finish:	1st, Indianapolis 500
IRL Season Earnings:	$ 1,446,854
IRL Pole Positions:	1, Indy 200

2nd PLACE
DAVY JONES

#70 Delco Electronics High Tech Team Galles
Entrant: Galles Racing International Crew Chief: Mitch Davis

Davy Jones came to Indianapolis with Galles Racing International as a veteran driver with an established team. On Race Day, Jones became a major player in the route to victory for the 80th running of the Indianapolis 500.

By Thursday of pole week, Jones had reached 231.696 miles per hour in practice. He became the month's fourth qualifier with an impressive four-lap run of 232.882, with a best lap of 233.064 and was the first to break Roberto Guerrero's four-year-old track records. Just 14 minutes later, Tony Stewart snapped both marks.

He started second alongside Stewart and trailed the latter into the first turn when the green flag dropped. Before the race was over, he led five times for 46 laps. On one restart, he brushed the inside wall on the front straightaway trying to pass Eliseo Salazar, but recovered to take command with 10 laps to go.

But on Lap 192, Buddy Lazier passed him on the frontstretch and Jones couldn't catch him on a late restart. At the end, he was just .695 of a second away of going to Victory Lane.

"On my restart, I would've liked to have been just a little bit better, maybe," he added. "I could have gotten by Michel Jourdain (who was between Jones and Lazier) on the front straightaway. Then it would have been myself and Buddy on the back straightaway. But as it was, I got caught up in Turn 2 on the last lap.

"Perhaps if there was one more lap, things could've been different."

1996 INDY 500 PERFORMANCE PROFILE

Starting Position:	2
Qualifying Average:	232.882 MPH
Qualifying Speed Rank:	4
Best Practice Speed:	234.736 MPH 5/11
Total Practice Laps:	240
Number Practice Days:	7
Finishing Position:	2
Laps Completed:	200 147.948 MPH
Highest Position 1996 Race:	1
Fastest Race Lap:	152 230.734 MPH
1996 Prize Money:	$ 632,503
INDY 500 Career Earnings:	$ 1,257,599
Career INDY 500 Starts:	4
Career Best Finish:	2nd 1996

1996 IRL PERFORMANCE PROFILE

IRL Points Championship:	21st, 33 points
IRL Best Finish:	2nd, Indianapolis 500
IRL Season Earnings:	$ 632,503

1995 REYNARD/FORD COSWORTH V8
GOODYEAR

3rd PLACE
RICHIE
HEARN

#4 Della Penna Motorsports Ralph's Food 4 Less Fuji Film
Entrant: Della Penna Motorsports   Crew Chief: Brendon Cleave

Richie Hearn came to the Indy Racing League with his Atlantic series team of Della Penna Motorsports.

He qualified for the front row for the Indy 200, but a tangle with Eddie Cheever relegated him to a backup car at the rear of the field.

Starting 19th, he was seventh by the 17th circuit around the one-mile oval. But he hit the wall in Turn 2 and finished 19th.

It was on to Phoenix, where he qualified for his second front row, setting a track record before Arie Luyendyk broke it 21 minutes later. He finished fourth, leading seven laps of the race and turning the lead over when he spun on a restart.

It was on to the Speedway, where he was among the initial group to pass driver's tests. On Day 6, he reached 231.941 miles per hour in practice. He became the seventh qualifier of the month at a four-lap average of 226.521, winding up 15th in the starting lineup.

In the race, he reached second place by Lap 166 and stayed among the leaders at the end. He finished third, the last driver on the lead lap.

"I was pretty amazed," Hearn said. "It's pretty awesome, looking down the track, three rows of cars and all of the people. This is not a disappointment to me. It took me the first 50 laps to get used to the turbulence and how much rev I had. I made passes I didn't think I'd ever get to make. The mental part is the toughest part. I was really getting into it."

1996 INDY 500 PERFORMANCE PROFILE

Starting Position:	15
Qualifying Average:	226.521 MPH
Qualifying Speed Rank:	20
Best Practice Speed:	234.308 MPH 5/11
Total Practice Laps:	824
Number Practice Days:	12
Finishing Position:	3
Laps Completed:	200 147.871 MPH
Highest Position 1996 Race:	2
Fastest Race Lap:	113 229.516 MPH
1996 Prize Money:	$ 375,203
INDY 500 Career Earnings:	$ 375,203
Career INDY 500 Starts:	1
Career Best Finish:	3rd 1996

1996 IRL PERFORMANCE PROFILE

IRL Points Championship:	3rd, 237 points
IRL Best Finish:	3rd, Indianapolis 500
IRL Season Earnings:	$ 512,203

1995 LOLA/FORD COSWORTH XB
GOODYEAR

#8 Mi-Jack/AGIP/Xcel

Entrant: Team Scandia   Crew Chief: Jack Pegues

Alessandro Zampedri came to the Speedway as a veteran with Team Scandia and a chance to win.

The young Italian driver was the fourth of the month to qualify when Pole Day arrived, putting together a four-lap average of 229.595 miles per hour for seventh starting position.

"This run was a couple of miles an hour slower than what I wanted," he said, "but I'm seeing everybody a little slower today. There was a lot of wind in Turn 2. It hit me at a 45-degree angle and it felt like someone was pushing me down. Because of the stands on the front stretch, you can't feel it. We just didn't have enough time because of the rain. We're a little behind schedule."

On the final practice day, Zampedri ran a comfortable 220.864 with a Race Day setup in just 13 laps.

As the race progressed, he stayed in sight of the leaders until his turn came on Lap 170 after Davy Jones brushed the wall on a restart and Zampedri took command.

He stayed in front for 20 laps until Jones reclaimed the edge in Turn 4. On the final restart, Zampedri became involved in the Turn 4 tangle with Eliseo Salazar and Roberto Guerrero and suffered severe leg, ankle and foot fractures. He still finished fourth.

He was destined to undergo surgery several times to repair the damage, but was determined to walk again — and race again — as summer turned to fall.

1996 INDY 500 PERFORMANCE PROFILE

Starting Position:	7
Qualifying Average:	229.595 MPH
Qualifying Speed Rank:	10
Best Practice Speed:	231.672 MPH 5/13
Total Practice Laps:	372
Number Practice Days:	7
Finishing Position:	4
Laps Completed:	199 147.653 MPH
Highest Position 1996 Race:	1
Fastest Race Lap:	189 226.392 MPH
1996 Prize Money:	$ 270,853
INDY 500 Career Earnings:	$ 438,253
Career INDY 500 Starts:	2
Career Best Finish:	4th 1996

1996 IRL PERFORMANCE PROFILE

IRL Points Championship:	23rd, 31 points
IRL Best Finish:	4th, Indianapolis 500
IRL Season Earnings:	$ 270,853

5th PLACE
ROBERTO GUERRERO

#21 WavePhore/Pennzoil Reynard-Ford
Entrant: Pagan Racing   Crew Chief: John Barnes

Roberto Guerrero came to the Indy Racing League's inaugural campaign as one of its seasoned veterans.

He started on the front row for the Indy 200 at Walt Disney World after Richie Hearn crashed in practice and was forced to use another car and start at the rear. Ironically, the car Hearn used was Guerrero's backup for Pagan Racing. The popular veteran drove a steady race to finish in fifth.

It was on to the Dura-Lube 200 at Phoenix, where he qualified third and finished 16th as a result of a damaged CV joint from a Turn 3 incident with Fermin Velez.

At Indianapolis, Guerrero stayed among the front runners in practice, reaching 232.336 miles per hour on Day 4. He put together a four-lap average of 231.373 on Pole Day to wind up in sixth starting position. But he had lost his one- and four-lap track records.

"It was an honor holding the record for four years but it's time I gave it up," he said. "This year, it was inevitable. Holding the record has been a weight. With the new rules, it'll be difficult to break the record again."

In the race, he led three times for a total of 47 laps, tops among all drivers, but was slowed in his bid by a long fuel stop. On the final-lap restart, he spun in Turn 4 coming to the flag and wound up in a tangle with Alessandro Zampedri and Eliseo Salazar. He finished sixth, two laps off the pace.

1996 INDY 500 PERFORMANCE PROFILE

Starting Position:	6
Qualifying Average:	231.373 MPH
Qualifying Speed Rank:	8
Best Practice Speed:	234.308 MPH 5/13
Total Practice Laps:	186
Number Practice Days:	6
Finishing Position:	5
Laps Completed:	198 146.905 MPH
Highest Position 1996 Race:	1
Fastest Race Lap:	145 230.503 MPH
1996 Prize Money:	$ 315,503
INDY 500 Career Earnings:	$ 2,178,763
Career INDY 500 Starts:	11
Career Best Finish:	2nd 1984 & 1987

1996 IRL PERFORMANCE PROFILE

IRL Points Championship:	3rd, 237 points
IRL Best Finish:	5th, Indianapolis 500
IRL Season Earnings:	$ 439,503

6th PLACE
ELISEO
SALAZAR

#7 Cristal/Copec Mobil
Entrant: Team Scandia   Crew Chief: David Jacobs

Eliseo Salazar had been a veteran adviser to the young Indy Racing League drivers when the IRL went on its maiden voyage at Orlando, counseling them in rookie meetings on what to expect of the new track at Walt Disney World.

But in practice the day before the Indy 200, he hit the wall off the fourth turn and slid the length of the front straight before whacking the outside wall and suffering a severe thigh fracture. He was out of action until the circuit moved to the Speedway and he was determined to make up for lost time.

Salazar reached a speed of 232.558 miles per hour in practice before Pole Day. As the 14th qualifier for the "500," he registered a four-lap run of 232.684 and wound up with a starting spot on the outside of the front row.

"Three months ago, I was in intensive care and I tried to get out of bed and fainted," Salazar said. "I just wanted to get back and race and to be here, and in the front row so far, is like a dream. During the rehab, I had the motivation to get back here. I knew I could do it and I was crying after my laps in the car."

In the race, he survived a contact with Arie Luyendyk in the south warmup lane and stayed with the front runners. But on the final lap, he was involved in the fourth-turn incident with Roberto Guerrero and Alessandro Zampedri, suffered a bruised right knee and finished sixth, three laps down.

1996 INDY 500 PERFORMANCE PROFILE

Starting Position:	3
Qualifying Average:	232.684 MPH
Qualifying Speed Rank:	5
Best Practice Speed:	234.858 MPH 5/13
Total Practice Laps:	463
Number Practice Days:	9
Finishing Position:	6
Laps Completed:	197 146.148 MPH
Highest Position 1996 Race:	2
Fastest Race Lap:	25 227.940 MPH
1996 Prize Money:	$ 226,653
INDY 500 Career Earnings:	$ 447,253
Career INDY 500 Starts:	2
Career Best Finish:	4th 1995

1996 IRL PERFORMANCE PROFILE

IRL Points Championship:	18th, 58 points
IRL Best Finish:	6th, Indianapolis 500
IRL Season Earnings:	$ 236,653

7th PLACE
DANNY ONGAIS

1995 LOLA/MENARD V6
FIRESTONE

#32 Glidden Menards Special
Entrant: Team Menard, Inc.   Crew Chief: Kevin Blanch

Danny Ongais came to the Speedway in search of a ride for a bid to make the "500" field for the first time since 1986.

He made his first appearance on the track on Day 13 in a Brickell Racing entry. On Day 14, the last practice day before the final qualification weekend, he had the car up to 208.459 miles per hour.

The next day, while others prepared to qualify, Ongais was passing his 20-lap refresher. But at 11 a.m. on the final qualifying day, the announcement was made that Ongais would drive the car qualified by the late Scott Brayton for the pole.

"These are rather large shoes to fill and I'll do my best for Team Menard," Ongais said. "I'm not familiar with all the situation but it's a difficult time. I knew Scott for a few years. We knew each other well enough to say hello...the friendship was there."

On Race Day, Ongais started in 33rd spot as a substitute driver. He finished seventh, his highest placing of the day, despite a half-spin in Turn 3 which brought out the caution for Laps 18-20.

"It was a great race car," Ongais said. "It was fantastic. I made a couple mistakes during the day. I killed the engine on a pit stop one time and then killed it on a restart. I feel great. The rookies moved over and gave you room when you needed it. I had no problems whatsoever."

1996 INDY 500 PERFORMANCE PROFILE

Starting Position:	33
Qualifying Average:	233.718 MPH
Qualifying Speed Rank:	2
Best Practice Speed:	226.364 MPH 5/23
Total Practice Laps:	107
Number Practice Days:	4
Finishing Position:	7
Laps Completed:	197 145.659 MPH
Highest Position 1996 Race:	7
Fastest Race Lap:	154 229.545 MPH
1996 Prize Money:	$ 228,253
INDY 500 Career Earnings:	$ 694,359
Career INDY 500 Starts:	10
Career Best Finish:	4th 1976

1996 IRL PERFORMANCE PROFILE

IRL Points Championship:	24th, 28 points
IRL Best Finish:	7th, Indianapolis 500
IRL Season Earnings:	$ 228,253

1994 LOLA/FORD COSWORTH XB FIRESTONE

HIDESHI
MATSUDA

#52 Team Taisan/Beck Motorsports
Entrant: Beck Motorsports   Crew Chief: Tom Bose

Hideshi Matsuda took Beck Motorsports' 1994 Lola out for the first time on the morning of the final time-trial day, his own first appearance of the month on the track.

He quickly reached 227.147 miles per hour by 1:35 p.m. When the Beck team pushed the car in the qualifying line at 4:02 p.m., he had logged only 35 practice laps. But he breezed to a four-lap average of 226.856 miles per hour to go solidly into the field.

"I'm so happy right now," Matsuda said. "I have to work with the car a little more and get more comfortable. I try to remember how I was last year and try to duplicate it. Going into Turn 2 (on Lap 3), the car had a little push and I tried to correct it, went out of control and corrected it...a little bit scared. (I) used (the) full course to recover.

"I love Indy. Four years ago, I came here as a pit reporter. I was touched by the speed, the sound of the cars, everything, and wanted to drive here. I went back to Japan and put a resume together to get a sponsor to come here. I am so happy to be here."

He started 30th and worked his way to eighth at the finish.

"At the beginning, I was worried about the accident last year," Matsuda said. "I didn't want to repeat what happened so I was watching in my rear-view mirror. The car was understeering a little bit during the whole race but I finished in the top 10, so I'm very happy."

1996 INDY 500 PERFORMANCE PROFILE

Starting Position:	30
Qualifying Average:	226.856 MPH
Qualifying Speed Rank:	19
Best Practice Speed:	227.192 MPH 5/19
Total Practice Laps:	63
Number Practice Days:	2
Finishing Position:	8
Laps Completed:	197 145.619 MPH
Highest Position 1996 Race:	8
Fastest Race Lap:	169 221.976 MPH
1996 Prize Money:	$ 233,953
INDY 500 Career Earnings:	$ 584,818
Career INDY 500 Starts:	2
Career Best Finish:	8th 1996

1996 IRL PERFORMANCE PROFILE

IRL Points Championship:	25th, 27 points
IRL Best Finish:	8th, Indianapolis 500
IRL Season Earnings:	$ 233,953

ROBBIE
BUHL

1994 LOLA/FORD COSWORTH XB
FIRESTONE

#54 Original Coors/Beck Motorsports
Entrant: Beck Motorsports   Crew Chief: Chris Beck

Robbie Buhl joined Beck Motorsports for the first Indy Racing League season and took the team to the front for each of the series' first two races — the only driver other than Tony Stewart to do so.

Buhl qualified 13th for the Indy 200 at Walt Disney World, led the 73rd lap and got his best championship finish with third.

"I got my first 200-lap race in," Buhl said. "I was just happy to be up front. I was proud to be a part of the team. We were giving our-selves some margin out there and not taking too many risks. We had a pretty clean race."

For the Dura-Lube 200 at Phoenix, he quali-fied 13th and went to the front twice for 20 laps but bowed out with a header problem, finishing 13th.

"What I really wanted was a top five and if a podium presented itself, it would've been great," Buhl said. "The crew had given me the opportu-nity to win. We're all frustrated right now but hopefully we can make up for it next race."

That would be the Indianapolis 500, where he qualified for 23rd starting spot on the sec-ond day at a four-lap average of 226.217. He was in his first Indianapolis 500 field.

"When I fell in love with racing was when I came here at seven years old," Buhl said. "That's why I'm in racing, because of the first time I came here."

On Race Day, he ran as high as fifth before finishing ninth, three laps down.

1996 INDY 500 PERFORMANCE PROFILE

Starting Position:	23
Qualifying Average:	226.217 MPH
Qualifying Speed Rank:	21
Best Practice Speed:	227.049 MPH 5/12
Total Practice Laps:	244
Number Practice Days:	4
Finishing Position:	9
Laps Completed:	197 145.615 MPH
Highest Position 1996 Race:	5
Fastest Race Lap:	61 218.155 MPH
1996 Prize Money:	$ 195,403
INDY 500 Career Earnings:	$ 195,403
Career INDY 500 Starts:	1
Career Best Finish:	9th 1996

1996 IRL PERFORMANCE PROFILE

IRL Points Championship:	2nd, 240 points
IRL Best Finish:	3rd, Indy 200
IRL Season Earnings:	$ 351,153

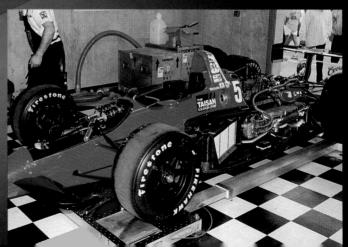

1995 LOLA/FORD COSWORTH XB
GOODYEAR

SCOTT SHARP

#11 Conseco AJ Foyt Racing
Entrant: AJ Foyt Enterprises   Crew Chief: John King

Scott Sharp joined A.J. Foyt Enterprises and qualified fourth for the inaugural Indy 200 at Walt Disney World but wound up 11th after a first-turn tangle with Eddie Cheever.

From there, it was on to Phoenix and the Dura-Lube 200. He was sixth fastest in qualifying and got his best career championship finish by winding up just 8.896 seconds behind winner Arie Luyendyk in second...despite a penalty for entering a closed pit.

Still, it was on to Indianapolis and a shot at the first IRL championship.

He qualified 21st on the second day after a Pole Day waveoff, posting a four-lap average of 231.201 miles per hour.

"This feels good to get in the show today," Sharp said. "We're going to plan on running to the front early, because if you wait very long, the leaders can get away from you. We thought we had a shot at one of the top two rows until the engine problems yesterday."

On Race Day, he charged to the front, reaching fourth place by Lap 36. His day ended after 194 laps in an accident in Turn 2. But he finished 10th, good enough to claim a share of the IRL title with Buzz Calkins.

"The team has done such a great job," Sharp said. "They really deserve the credit. We've been fast everywhere we've gone. I think this series can go to the moon. It really shines. This is a unique championship. There's only one time you can be a first champion of the IRL."

1996 INDY 500 PERFORMANCE PROFILE

Starting Position:	21
Qualifying Average:	231.201 MPH
Qualifying Speed Rank:	9
Best Practice Speed:	235.701 MPH 5/10
Total Practice Laps:	225
Number Practice Days:	10
Finishing Position:	10
Laps Completed:	194 148.420 MPH
Highest Position 1996 Race:	4
Fastest Race Lap:	151 228.131 MPH
1996 Prize Money:	$ 202,053
INDY 500 Career Earnings:	$ 521,719
Career INDY 500 Starts:	2
Career Best Finish:	10th 1996

1996 IRL PERFORMANCE PROFILE

IRL Points Championship:	1st, 246 points
IRL Best Finish:	2nd, Dura-Lube 200
IRL Season Earnings:	$ 361,303

11th PLACE
EDDIE
CHEEVER

1995 LOLA/MENARD V6
FIRESTONE

#3 Quaker State Menards Special
Entrant: Team Menard, Inc.   Crew Chief: Steve Melson

Eddie Cheever was on hand for the announcement of the new track at Walt Disney World, participated in the "formation run" for the track's dedication and was in the fold with Team Menard at the inaugural Indy 200.

He had already qualified when a final-practice collision with Richie Hearn sent both to the back of the pack for the Indy 200 start. A Turn 1 accident with Scott Sharp led him 10th for the day.

In practice for the Dura-Lube 200 at Phoenix, bad luck bit him again and he hit the Turn 4 wall, suffered a concussion and was ruled out for the weekend.

At Indianapolis, the outlook turned brighter, as Cheever, teammate Tony Stewart and Arie Luyendyk put up big numbers during practice. Cheever reached 235.997 miles per hour on Day 4 and was the 12th qualifier of the month when he reeled off a four-lap average of 231.781.

On Race Day, after starting fourth, he was running among the leaders until trouble struck. After returning, he ran 22 of the fastest 50 laps of the race, including the fastest one ever run in the race in Speedway history at 236.103. His determined ride left him 11th at the end, 11 laps down.

"I think I had the best car," Cheever said. "I had a pit-stop problem in the very beginning and I went sideways. I just couldn't get a yellow. The engine broke in the end."

1996 INDY 500 PERFORMANCE PROFILE

Starting Position:	4
Qualifying Average:	231.781 MPH
Qualifying Speed Rank:	6
Best Practice Speed:	235.997 MPH 5/07
Total Practice Laps:	217
Number Practice Days:	7
Finishing Position:	11
Laps Completed:	189 145.338 MPH
Highest Position 1996 Race:	5
Fastest Race Lap:	78 236.103 MPH
1996 Prize Money:	$ 206,103
INDY 500 Career Earnings:	$ 1,352,652
Career INDY 500 Starts:	6
Career Best Finish:	4th 1992

1996 IRL PERFORMANCE PROFILE

IRL Points Championship:	13th, 147 points
IRL Best Finish:	10th, Indy 200
IRL Season Earnings:	$ 281,353

1995 LOLA/FORD COSWORTH XB
GOODYEAR

#14 AJ Foyt Copenhagen Racing
Entrant: AJ Foyt Enterprises   Crew Chief: Craig Baranouski

Hamilton

Davey Hamilton and Scott Sharp became teammates for A.J. Foyt Enterprises to go into the Indy 200 at Walt Disney World, which would be Davey's first championship-car race.

As things turned out, the veteran West Coast supermodified driver led two laps of the race before a Turn 2 crash left him in 12th place.

From there, it was on to Phoenix for the Dura-Lube 200 at a track where he had won Copper World Classic features in three different classes of cars. After qualifying ninth, he finished 17th, sidelined by electrical problems after 77 laps.

It was on to Indy and he became the month's 11th qualifier at a four-lap average of 228.887 miles per hour, solidly in his first "500" field in 10th starting spot.

"We wanted to run over 230 but we didn't quite make it," Hamilton said. "That's all right because we have a good race setup. After last year, there was a lot of pressure on me. It's been a dream of mine to get in the race and getting in is a load off my shoulders."

On Race Day, he moved to fourth place on Lap 38 and wound up in 12th place, running at the end.

"I'm glad we finished," Hamilton said. "It's a little disappointing. Th car wasn't as good as I thought it would be. The back end was loose and we burned up a bearing. We were fortunate not to hit the wall. This is my first Indy. It was a great experience. I'll be back next year."

1996 INDY 500 PERFORMANCE PROFILE

Starting Position:	10
Qualifying Average:	228.887 MPH
Qualifying Speed Rank:	13
Best Practice Speed:	230.864 MPH 5/10
Total Practice Laps:	209
Number Practice Days:	9
Finishing Position:	12
Laps Completed:	181 133.790 MPH
Highest Position 1996 Race:	4
Fastest Race Lap:	32 220.951 MPH
1996 Prize Money:	$ 184,003
INDY 500 Career Earnings:	$ 184,003
Career INDY 500 Starts:	1
Career Best Finish:	12th 1996

1996 IRL PERFORMANCE PROFILE

IRL Points Championship:	7th, 192 points
IRL Best Finish:	12th, Indianapolis 500
IRL Season Earnings:	$ 286,503

13th PLACE
MICHEL
JOURDAIN, JR.

1995 LOLA/FORD COSWORTH V8
GOODYEAR

#22 Herdez Quaker State/Viva Mexico!
Entrant: Team Scandia   Crew Chief: John Weiland

At age 19, Jourdain was the youngest to join the new League, getting a Team Scandia ride for the Dura-Lube 200 at Phoenix. He qualified for 14th starting spot. He finished 20th, sidelined by a Turn 4 accident, but he had taken his first step toward Indianapolis.

Jourdain was one of the first group to pass the driver's test on Day 3 of the month of May and reached third fastest among the newcomers on that day at 228.154 miles per hour behind Tony Stewart and Mark Dismore.

Even when the veterans joined them on the track, Jourdain was 10th quickest on Day 6 at 229.142. And when Pole Day came, he ran a four-lap average of 229.380, good for eighth starting spot and $7,500 from Ameritech as the youngest starting driver.

"It's a dream come true," he said. "Now we have to work on the car for the race. The whole team did a great job."

He stayed near the top 10 before mechanical problems left him 13th. On the last-lap restart, he was, uneventfully, between Buddy Lazier and Davy Jones as the pair battled for the victory.

"The right rear wheel bearing broke during the race and after that, we were in the pits a long time and not able to catch up," Jourdain said. "We're happy that we finished the race. I hope next year we can make this up. We were in a good position and we took the checkered, which is important. We could've been fifth or sixth, but that's racing."

1996 INDY 500 PERFORMANCE PROFILE

Starting Position:	8
Qualifying Average:	229.380 MPH
Qualifying Speed Rank:	11
Best Practice Speed:	234.223 MPH 5/13
Total Practice Laps:	325
Number Practice Days:	7
Finishing Position:	13
Laps Completed:	177 130.918 MPH
Highest Position 1996 Race:	6
Fastest Race Lap:	122 225.096 MPH
1996 Prize Money:	$ 193,653
INDY 500 Career Earnings:	$ 193,653
Career INDY 500 Starts:	1
Career Best Finish:	13th 1996

1996 IRL PERFORMANCE PROFILE

IRL Points Championship:	16th, 74 points
IRL Best Finish:	13th, Indianapolis 500
IRL Season Earnings:	$ 247,403

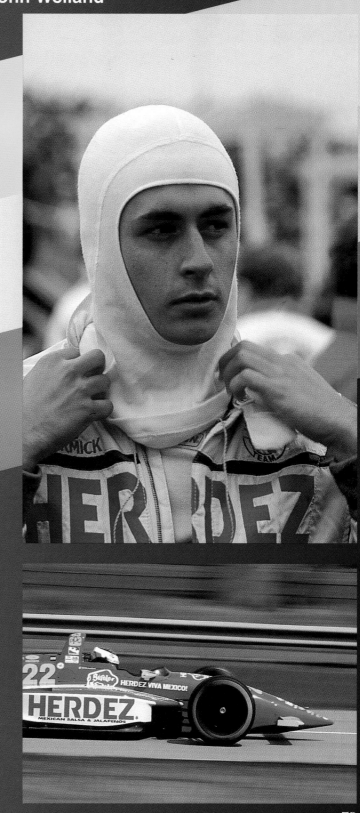

1994 LOLA/FORD COSWORTH XB
FIRESTONE

14th PLACE
LYN
ST. JAMES

#45 Spirit of San Antonio
Entrant: Zunne Group Racing   Crew Chief: Phil McRobert

Lyn St. James qualified 11th for the inaugural Indy 200 and drove a steady race to eighth in a Team Scandia machine.

It was on to the Dura-Lube 200 at Phoenix, where misfortune awaited. Again with Team Scandia, Buddy Lazier collected her in Turn 2 during practice after a mechanical malfunction on Lazier's car.

"He passed me inside and cleared me," St. James said. "He went low, then the back end came around."

She started a backup car in 22nd, but finished 21st, bowing out after 11 laps with electrical problems.

Next came Indianapolis, and St. James was without a ride in the first few days of May. But on Day 4, Zunne Group Racing announced St. James would drive its entry fielded by McCormack Motorsports. On Pole Day, she was the first qualifier of the month at a four-lap average of 224.594 miles per hour.

"There's not going to be an eight mile-per-hour difference in the race," St. James said. "I feel we're looking at the fastest speeds we've ever driven at this track. It's a different surface and tire composition and structure. We're not running on the ragged edge or risking anything."

After starting 18th, she ran as high as 12th before a tangle with Scott Harrington in Turn 1 left her on the sidelines with a broken wrist and a 14th-place finish.

1996 INDY 500 PERFORMANCE PROFILE

Starting Position:	18
Qualifying Average:	224.594 MPH
Qualifying Speed Rank:	26
Best Practice Speed:	226.992 MPH 5/16
Total Practice Laps:	223
Number Practice Days:	8
Finishing Position:	14
Laps Completed:	153 139.365 MPH
Highest Position 1996 Race:	12
Fastest Race Lap:	41 214.756 MPH
1996 Prize Money:	$ 182,603
INDY 500 Career Earnings:	$ 835,974
Career INDY 500 Starts:	4
Career Best Finish:	11th 1992

1996 IRL PERFORMANCE PROFILE

IRL Points Championship:	9th, 186 points
IRL Best Finish:	8th, Indy 200
IRL Season Earnings:	$ 264,853

15th PLACE
SCOTT
HARRINGTON

1995 REYNARD/FORD COSWORTH V8
GOODYEAR

#44 Gold Eagle/Mechanics Laundry/Harrington/LP
Entrant: Della Penna Motorsports   Crew Chief: Brendon Cleave

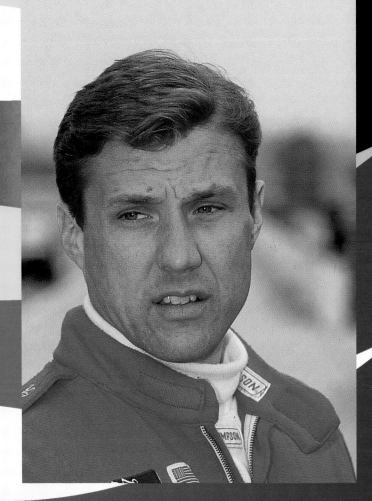

Scott Harrington and LP Racing acquired a car and became one of the last entries for the 80th running of the race, filing just before the deadline. He had passed his driver's test in 1989 and had not returned to the Speedway in seven years.

He passed the final observation phase of his driver's test on Day 13, just before the final weekend of time trials. Just moments later, however, he hit the Turn 4 wall, suffering a bruised left foot and left shoulder.

Things looked bleak for the team, until it was able to put together a last-minute deal with Della Penna Motorsports for a backup car to Richie Hearn. With just 23 minutes remaining in qualifications, Harrington put the machine in the show at a four-lap average of 222.185 miles per hour.

On Race Day, after starting 32nd, Scott worked his way to 13th, despite an early race spin. But he tangled with Lyn St. James in Turn 1 to end his day in 15th.

"I was coming up on her and the next thing I knew, she was right on top of me," Harrington said. "I went down on the grass trying to give her room. She didn't see me. It's just racing, I guess. It's just real disappointing. We worked so hard to get here. We had problems at the start. I spun the car right off the bat. It was 100 percent my fault. But we had just started making some strides and were picking up some speed."

1996 INDY 500 PERFORMANCE PROFILE

Starting Position:	32
Qualifying Average:	222.185 MPH
Qualifying Speed Rank:	33
Best Practice Speed:	225.807 MPH 5/19
Total Practice Laps:	208
Number Practice Days:	5
Finishing Position:	15
Laps Completed:	150 136.631 MPH
Highest Position 1996 Race:	13
Fastest Race Lap:	134 215.136 MPH
1996 Prize Money:	$ 190,753
INDY 500 Career Earnings:	$ 190,753
Career INDY 500 Starts:	1
Career Best Finish:	15th 1996

1996 IRL PERFORMANCE PROFILE

IRL Points Championship:	26th, 20 points
IRL Best Finish:	15th, Indianapolis 500
IRL Season Earnings:	$ 190,753

#5 Jonathan Byrd's Cafeteria/Bryant Heating & Cooling
Entrant: Jonathan Byrd/Treadway Racing   Crew Chief: Brad McCanless

Arie Luyendyk captured the third starting spot at the Indy 200 at Walt Disney World, finishing 14th when gearbox problems plagued the Byrd/Treadway team.

From there, he began a record-breaking journey, starting with the pole position for the Dura-Lube 200 at Phoenix with a track record speed of 183.599 miles per hour. He parlayed the starting spot into a dominating victory, leading four times for 122 laps and beating runner-up Scott Sharp by 8.896 seconds.

It was on to Indianapolis, and Luyendyk battled the Menard team for practice supremacy, winning that war with the fastest practice lap ever at the Speedway at 239.260 miles per hour on Day 7. With Tony Stewart on the pole, Luyendyk reeled off a four-lap average of 233.390 to wrest away the top spot. Although the late Scott Brayton later bested him, Luyendyk's run was disallowed, causing him to qualify on the second day.

On his second run in a different car, he broke Brayton's new records with a top lap of 237.498 and a four-lap average of 236.986. That gave him practice, one- and four-lap records to go with his 1990 race record of 185.981.

The run gave him 20th starting position. During the race, he moved up quickly and was eighth by Lap 10 and second by Lap 97. But contact with Eliseo Salazar in the south warmup lane damaged Luyendyk's machine beyond immediate repair.

1996 INDY 500 PERFORMANCE PROFILE

Starting Position:	20
Qualifying Average:	236.986 MPH
Qualifying Speed Rank:	1
Best Practice Speed:	239.260 MPH 5/10
Total Practice Laps:	400
Number Practice Days:	11
Finishing Position:	16
Laps Completed:	149 139.432 MPH
Highest Position 1996 Race:	2
Fastest Race Lap:	62 232.931 MPH
1996 Prize Money:	$ 216,503
INDY 500 Career Earnings:	$ 3,459,179
Career INDY 500 Starts:	11
Career Best Finish:	1st 1990

1996 IRL PERFORMANCE PROFILE

IRL Points Championship:	5th, 225 points
IRL Best Finish:	1st, Dura-Lube 200
IRL Season Earnings:	$ 414,003
IRL Pole Positions:	1, Dura-Lube 200

17th PLACE
BUZZ
CALKINS

1995 REYNARD/FORD COSWORTH XB
FIRESTONE

#12 Bradley Food Marts/Hoosier Lottery
Entrant: Bradley Motorsports   Crew Chief: Steve Ritenour

Buzz Calkins became the inaugural Indy 200's highest starting rookie, in fifth, when Richie Hearn had to move to the rear because of an accident during final practice. Calkins took his first lead on Lap 66 and command for good on Lap 76, leading 130 of the 200 circuits around the one-mile oval and holding back Tony Stewart in a fierce duel at the finish by .866 of a second.

From there, he took the IRL point lead to Phoenix for the Dura-Lube 200, started eighth and finished sixth to keep the point lead going to Indianapolis.

At the Speedway, on Pole Day, he became the ninth qualifier of the month at a four-lap average of 229.013 miles per hour. He had reached 234.693 in practice.

"I don't think we're ecstatic but we'll take it," Calkins said. "We're in the show. We lost a lot of time and I don't know why. (To be in the race) feels great. Obviously, this is a dream come true even though we didn't qualify as quickly as we liked. There's no place I'd rather be."

On Race Day, he started ninth and ran as high as sixth before brake gremlins struck, putting him on the sidelines after 148 laps in 17th place, watching Scott Sharp and others continue the charge for the first IRL championship. Sharp bowed out in an accident but his finishing position of 11th left he and Calkins to share the inaugural IRL driver title.

1996 INDY 500 PERFORMANCE PROFILE

Starting Position:	9
Qualifying Average:	229.013 MPH
Qualifying Speed Rank:	12
Best Practice Speed:	234.693 MPH 5/10
Total Practice Laps:	486
Number Practice Days:	9
Finishing Position:	17
Laps Completed:	148 138.430 MPH
Highest Position 1996 Race:	6
Fastest Race Lap:	88 226.199 MPH
1996 Prize Money:	$ 173,553
INDY 500 Career Earnings:	$ 173,553
Career INDY 500 Starts:	1
Career Best Finish:	17th 1996

1996 IRL PERFORMANCE PROFILE

IRL Points Championship:	1st, 246 points
IRL Best Finish:	1st, Indy 200
IRL Season Earnings:	$ 376,553

1993 LOLA/MENARD V6
FIRESTONE

Entrant: Team Blueprint Racing Inc.

#27 Team Blueprint Racing
Crew Chief: Tommy O'Brien

Jim Guthrie had raced go-karts, late-model stock cars, Formula Fords and Formula Atlantics in the past and was serving as president of Car Crafters Collision and treasurer of Albuquerque Christian School when an opportunity arose. He journeyed to Phoenix, where he joined forces with Team Blueprint for the Dura-Lube 200, his first race in a championship car.

Guthrie qualified for 18th starting spot as the fifth qualifier for the race and finished 13th, sidelined by a Turn 3 accident.

At the Speedway, he was among the first group on Day 3 to complete his driver's test. He qualified on Pole Day at a four-lap average of 222.394 miles per hour.

"I've run less than 150 laps all month long," Guthrie said, "and the fastest of those 150 were during qualifying. I can't think of a better way to spend a Saturday afternoon. Because of Tony George and the IRL, guys like me have a chance to run here. It's awesome. It's really cool."

On Race Day, he completed 144 laps before the engine failed. He had run as high as 11th after starting 19th.

"It just let go all of a sudden," Guthrie said. "We didn't get any warning. The car was getting better every segment. We had a bad push at the start but kept taking that push out a little at a time. The car got very easy to handle in traffic. It was very easy to pass. It was a drag something had to happen, but even with that, it was great. I'd do this again tomorrow."

1996 INDY 500 PERFORMANCE PROFILE

Starting Position:	19
Qualifying Average:	222.394 MPH
Qualifying Speed Rank:	31
Best Practice Speed:	222.502 MPH 5/11
Total Practice Laps:	180
Number Practice Days:	6
Finishing Position:	18
Laps Completed:	144 131.824 MPH
Highest Position 1996 Race:	11
Fastest Race Lap:	142 222.151 MPH
1996 Prize Money:	$ 168,453
INDY 500 Career Earnings:	$ 168,453
Career INDY 500 Starts:	1
Career Best Finish:	18th 1996

1996 IRL PERFORMANCE PROFILE

IRL Points Championship:	16th, 74 points
IRL Best Finish:	15th, Dura-Lube 200
IRL Season Earnings:	$ 206,453

MARK
DISMORE

1995 LOLA/MENARD V6
FIRESTONE

#30 Quaker State Menards Special
Entrant: Team Menard, Inc.   Crew Chief: Steve Melson

For Mark Dismore, the return to the Indianapolis Motor Speedway was considerably better than his previous experiences.

He joined Team Menard for pre-month of May testing and tested fast. When the time came for driver's tests, Dismore was one of the first up. He completed it on Day 3 in just 71 minutes; only Nigel Mansell has been known to do so.

Then he promptly got up to 228.566 miles per hour, trailing only teammate Tony Stewart's 237.336 on that day.

In practice Friday before Pole Day, he reached 232.702, seventh fastest of the day. And he became the 18th qualifier of the month at 227.260, good for 14th starting spot.

His first spot in the field was a warm reward from 1991, when he was seriously injured in a crash during practice.

"Now, I finally get a shot," Dismore said. "I'm feeling sincerity from the bottom of my heart. It's been bottled up for a long time. Ever since I was a little kid, I wanted to be here. If I hadn't gotten this opportunity, I'd feel like an incomplete person. This whole week has been a dream. It's just a magical place."

On Race Day, he was as high as seventh before engine failure relegated him to 19th.

However, he had made his mark. He had the seventh fastest lap of the race at 233.803.

1996 INDY 500 PERFORMANCE PROFILE

Starting Position:	14
Qualifying Average:	227.260 MPH
Qualifying Speed Rank:	18
Best Practice Speed:	232.702 MPH 5/10
Total Practice Laps:	183
Number Practice Days:	5
Finishing Position:	19
Laps Completed:	129 143.734 MPH
Highest Position 1996 Race:	7
Fastest Race Lap:	62 233.803 MPH
1996 Prize Money:	$ 161,253
INDY 500 Career Earnings:	$ 161,253
Career INDY 500 Starts:	1
Career Best Finish:	19th 1996

1996 IRL PERFORMANCE PROFILE

IRL Points Championship:	27th, 16 points
IRL Best Finish:	19th, Indianapolis 500
IRL Season Earnings:	$ 161,253

#60 Valvoline Cummins Craftsman Special
Entrant: Walker Racing   Crew Chief: Tim Broyles

Mike Groff started the inaugural IRL season as a last-minute driver for A.J. Foyt Enterprises and wound up with Walker Racing's effort at Indy.

He jumped into Foyt's third car for the Indy 200 at Walt Disney World as a teammate to Scott Sharp and Davey Hamilton and qualified 12th on the grid with little practice.

On Race Day, he drove to sixth at the finish.

"This was an 11th-hour situation," Groff said. "It's great to be back with A.J. Honestly, the deal came together Wednesday night. I only had about 100 laps in the car. We had trouble with one of our pit stops with a right front wheel nut and we lost three laps. After we got that, everything started coming together."

It came together even better at Phoenix, where he qualified seventh and finished third, one lap off the pace because of a penalty for entering a closed pit.

At Indianapolis, he put together a four-lap average of 228.704 miles per hour to nail down 11th starting spot.

"I'd have to say the IRL has created a great opportunity for a lot of guys who would never have had a chance in the past," Groff said. "I guess the bottom line is, you want to line yourself up with the best opportunity and team and I've been very fortunate with Derrick Walker."

On Race Day, he was fourth just past the halfway point before a pit fire ended his day in 20th place.

1996 INDY 500 PERFORMANCE PROFILE

Starting Position:	11
Qualifying Average:	228.704 MPH
Qualifying Speed Rank:	15
Best Practice Speed:	230.491 MPH 5/14
Total Practice Laps:	353
Number Practice Days:	8
Finishing Position:	20
Laps Completed:	122 141.591 MPH
Highest Position 1996 Race:	4
Fastest Race Lap:	59 225.558 MPH
1996 Prize Money:	$ 158,503
INDY 500 Career Earnings:	$ 455,605
Career INDY 500 Starts:	2
Career Best Finish:	20th 1996

1996 IRL PERFORMANCE PROFILE

IRL Points Championship:	4th, 228 points
IRL Best Finish:	3rd, Dura-Lube 200
IRL Season Earnings	$ 306,253

1995 LOLA/FORD COSWORTH XB
GOODYEAR

#34 Scandia/Xcel/Royal Purple
Entrant: Team Scandia   Crew Chief: David Jacobs

Fermin Velez came to the Speedway as part of the Team Scandia contingent on a patriotic note. He wanted to become the first Spaniard to make the field of the Indianapolis 500.

Velez started his quest at the Dura-Lube 200 at Phoenix, his first oval track race. He completed his driver's test at an open session in February, then qualified 19th on the starting grid. He finished 19th, sidelined in a tangle with Roberto Guerrero.

At the Speedway, he passed the driver's test on Day 11 and immediately set out to reach qualifying speed.

"The Indy 500 will be the biggest accomplishment in my career," said the international road racer.

His time came as the second qualifier on the third day of time trials, and he recorded a four-lap run of 222.487 miles per hour.

"Every lap I do, I get a little better," Velez said. "All I wanted was to be in the race because then I would be the first driver from Spain to be in the race. Now that I am, it's a big relief and I'm very happy. Finally, I made it."

After starting 28th, he moved as high as 13th before an engine fire ended his day and he finished 21st.

"We think the water hose broke between (Turns) 1 and 2," Velez said. "There was a bunch of smoke. I felt a lot of heat on my back. The engine just quit and I got out of the car as soon as possible."

1996 INDY 500 PERFORMANCE PROFILE

Starting Position:	28
Qualifying Average:	222.487 MPH
Qualifying Speed Rank:	30
Best Practice Speed:	223.392 MPH 5/18
Total Practice Laps:	191
Number Practice Days:	6
Finishing Position:	21
Laps Completed:	107 134.251 MPH
Highest Position 1996 Race:	13
Fastest Race Lap:	105 218.659 MPH
1996 Prize Money:	$ 176,653
INDY 500 Career Earnings:	$ 176,653
Career INDY 500 Starts:	1
Career Best Finish:	21st 1996

1996 IRL PERFORMANCE PROFILE

IRL Points Championship:	17th, 60 points
IRL Best Finish:	19th, Dura-Lube 200
IRL Season Earnings:	$ 210,653

1994 LOLA/FORD COSWORTH XB
GOODYEAR

#43 Scandia/Fanatics Only/Xcel
Entrant: Team Scandia   Crew Chief: John Martin

When the Indy Racing League hit the track for the first time, Oswego supermodified standout Joe Gosek realized he might have a shot at his dream to run the Indianapolis 500.

He came to the Indianapolis Motor Speedway and fulfilled one dream by taking practice laps in a car around the famed 2 1/2-mile oval, first with the Tempero-Giuffre team.

He became the 21st driver to pass the test on Day 14, running a fastest lap of 206.219, still nowhere close to what it would take to make the field.

On the third time-trial day, he jumped into a backup Team Scandia car and started working his way up to speed. And, with 18 minutes remaining in qualifications for the month, he reeled off a run in the machine to a four-lap average of 222.793, bumping Billy Boat.

"It hasn't sunk in yet," Gosek said. "That's for sure. The month has been unbelievable. I was entranced with the place when I got here. I'm here as a racer. I was given the opportunity through the IRL and that's who I'm dedicated to now. There's a lot of good racers out there and I'm one of 'em."

He started 31st in the field and had gained 10 spots at one point. But radiator problems ended his day after 106 laps and Gosek finished 22nd.

1996 INDY 500 PERFORMANCE PROFILE

Starting Position:	31
Qualifying Average:	222.793 MPH
Qualifying Speed Rank:	29
Best Practice Speed:	223.730 MPH 5/19
Total Practice Laps:	176
Number Practice Days:	10
Finishing Position:	22
Laps Completed:	106 112.739 MPH
Highest Position 1996 Race:	21
Fastest Race Lap:	23 207.799 MPH
1996 Prize Money:	$ 169,653
INDY 500 Career Earnings:	$ 169,653
Career INDY 500 Starts:	1
Career Best Finish:	22nd 1996

1996 IRL PERFORMANCE PROFILE

IRL Points Championship:	28th, 13 points
IRL Best Finish:	22nd, Indianapolis 500
IRL Season Earnings:	$ 169,653

23rd PLACE
BRAD
MURPHEY

1994 REYNARD/FORD COSWORTH XB
FIRESTONE

#10 Hemelgarn Racing-Delta Faucet-Firestone
Entrant: Hemelgarn Racing, Inc.   Crew Chief: Mark Shambarger

Brad Murphey returned to the sport after a long absence to join Hemelgarn Racing for the Indianapolis 500. The former bronco riding champion started his month of May quietly and continued that way as he built up speed for qualifying.

He was one of the first groups to pass his driver's test on the third day of practice and was 10th fastest among the newcomers that day with a lap at 209.035 miles per hour.

On the second day of qualifying, he went to the line but engine trouble struck on his first lap and he passed.

Two days later, he was tops among drivers still hoping to qualify with a lap at 228.612 and was also tops on each of the two days preceding the final weekend with laps at 225.875 on Day 13 of the month and 228.548 on Day 14.

Murphey was the third qualifier on the third time-trial day and put the Hemelgarn machine smoothly into the race at a four-lap average of 226.053.

"We'd like to be faster," he said. "We had some trouble with the boost...the heat does that. But I can't complain...it's awesome. Just to be a part of it is special."

On Race Day, after starting 26th, he moved up to 15th before brushing the Turn 2 wall and breaking the suspension.

1996 INDY 500 PERFORMANCE PROFILE

Starting Position:	26
Qualifying Average:	226.053 MPH
Qualifying Speed Rank:	23
Best Practice Speed:	228.612 MPH 5/14
Total Practice Laps:	369
Number Practice Days:	12
Finishing Position:	23
Laps Completed:	91 140.355 MPH
Highest Position 1996 Race:	15
Fastest Race Lap:	90 219.213 MPH
1996 Prize Money:	$ 177,853
INDY 500 Career Earnings:	$ 177,853
Career INDY 500 Starts:	1
Career Best Finish:	1st 1996

1996 IRL PERFORMANCE PROFILE

IRL Points Championship:	29th, 12 points
IRL Best Finish:	23rd, Indianapolis 500
IRL Season Earnings:	$ 177,853

#20 Menards/Glidden/Quaker State Special
Entrant: Team Menard, Inc.   Crew Chief: Bill Martin

Tony Stewart chased Buzz Calkins to the flag to make history in the Indy 200 at Walt Disney World. He dodged the cleanup from an accident to set the stage for the dramatic duel.

In all, Stewart led 27 laps of his first-ever race in a championship car.

In Phoenix for the Dura-Lube 200, Stewart qualified fourth and led again for 11 laps, before problems sidelined him in 11th.

At Indy on Day 3, during driver's tests, Tony reached 237.336 miles per hour, fastest unofficial rookie lap in Speedway history.

On Pole Day, he became the first rookie to set one- and four-lap track records since Teo Fabi in 1983 and the fifth in history with a run of 233.100.

Later, Arie Luyendyk bested his run and teammate Scott Brayton one-upped Luyendyk for the pole, pushing Stewart to the outside of the front row. But Luyendyk's run was disallowed and Brayton's tragic death left Stewart as the pole sitter.

On Race Day, he led immediately and became the third rookie to lead his first lap of competition at Indy. When he led Lap 24, it broke Fabi's rookie mark of leading consecutive laps from the start.

His ninth lap - 232.324 miles per hour -was the first race lap at more than 230 miles an hour. His next lap, at 234.412, broke that mark. But Stewart pulled to the pits on Lap 82.

"No one can take anything away from this race. I don't care who it is. This is the Indy 500 and there isn't anything like it."

1996 INDY 500 PERFORMANCE PROFILE

Starting Position:	1
Qualifying Average:	233.100 MPH
Qualifying Speed Rank:	3
Best Practice Speed:	237.336 MPH 5/06
Total Practice Laps:	304
Number Practice Days:	10
Finishing Position:	24
Laps Completed:	82 148.022 MPH
Highest Position 1996 Race:	1
Fastest Race Lap:	10 234.412 MPH
1996 Prize Money:	$ 222,053
INDY 500 Career Earnings:	$ 222,053
Career INDY 500 Starts:	1
Career Best Finish:	24th 1996

1996 IRL PERFORMANCE PROFILE

IRL Points Championship:	6th, 204 points
IRL Best Finish:	2nd, Indy 200
IRL Season Earnings:	$ 375,303
IRL Pole Positions:	1, Indianapolis 500

1994 LOLA/FORD COSWORTH XB
GOODYEAR

#90 Team Scandia/Slick Gardner Enterprises
Entrant: Team Scandia   Crew Chief: Stephen Wulff

Racin Gardner came to the Indianapolis Motor Speedway with a strong background in off-road and land-speed record cars.

He had taken some laps in a Tempero-Giuffre machine at Phoenix but an oil leak stalled completion of his driver's test during the third phase.

It was on to Indy and a switch to Team Scandia. Gardner breezed through the driver's test on the third day of practice and began quietly preparing for a qualification attempt.

That came with just three minutes remaining in the first weekend of time trials, when he put the entry into the field at a four-lap average of 224.453 miles per hour.

"That's about the fastest I've run all week," Gardner said. "It was getting pretty close to the end of the day so I decided I better pick the speed up if I was going to make the show. This morning, we had a little bit of a push and were only going about 210. But we worked with it and got it dialed in."

On Race Day, after starting 25th, he moved up three spots to 22nd before a brush with the wall damaged the suspension and he was on the sidelines after 76 laps.

"The car was pushing right from the start today," said Gardner. "During the second stop, we put in some front wing but when I got back up to speed, I went right into the wall and bent the right front control arm."

1996 INDY 500 PERFORMANCE PROFILE

Starting Position:	25
Qualifying Average:	224.453 MPH
Qualifying Speed Rank:	27
Best Practice Speed:	224.933 MPH 5/12
Total Practice Laps:	165
Number Practice Days:	3
Finishing Position:	25
Laps Completed:	76 125.776 MPH
Highest Position 1996 Race:	22
Fastest Race Lap:	62 214.475 MPH
1996 Prize Money:	$ 149,853
INDY 500 Career Earnings:	$ 149,853
Career INDY 500 Starts:	1
Career Best Finish:	25th 1996
IRL Points Championship:	26th 20 points

1996 IRL PERFORMANCE PROFILE

IRL Points Championship:	26th, 20 points
IRL Best Finish:	25th, Indianapolis 500
IRL Season Earnings:	$ 149,853

1994 LOLA/FORD COSWORTH XB
GOODYEAR

#41 AJ Foyt Enterprises

Entrant: AJ Foyt Enterprises   **Crew Chief: Craig Baranouski**

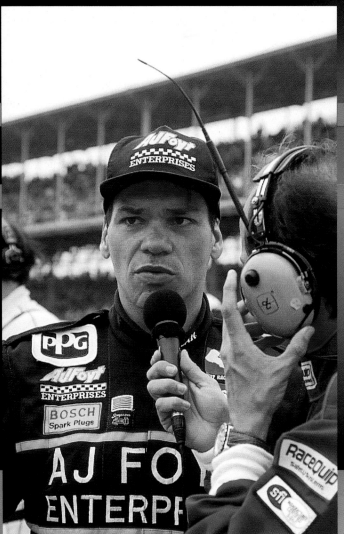

Marco Greco came to the Indianapolis Motor Speedway after getting a ride with A.J. Foyt Enterprises to bid for his second start at the "500."

He had bumped Scott Goodyear from the field in 1994 to gain his first "500'berth, but had waved off on five qualifying attempts — three in the last 33 minutes — to miss the show in 1995.

On Pole Day, he lost an engine in the morning practice. But he became the second qualifier on the second day of time trials with a four-lap average of 228.840 miles per hour, good for 22nd starting spot — in a 1994 Lola.

"It's great to be the fastest '94 car on the grid," Greco said. "I'm excited about that. Yesterday, we thought we had no problems but then the engine blew. So today is a big relief to be locked in the best race on the planet."

At the start of the race, Greco bided his time, moving up to 18th at one point. But eight laps later, on the leader's 64th circuit, engine failure struck again.

"The engine blew," Greco said. "I had over-steer. I hung on a little more. We made a pit stop to make changes. That's how motor racing goes, but it didn't work. To work with A.J. (Foyt) is a great honor for me."

1996 INDY 500 PERFORMANCE PROFILE

Starting Position:	22
Qualifying Average:	228.840 MPH
Qualifying Speed Rank:	14
Best Practice Speed:	229.481 MPH 5/12
Total Practice Laps:	225
Number Practice Days:	8
Finishing Position:	26
Laps Completed:	64 142.622 MPH
Highest Position 1996 Race:	18
Fastest Race Lap:	44 216.164 MPH
1996 Prize Money:	$ 153,303
INDY 500 Career Earnings:	$ 325,065
Career INDY 500 Starts:	2
Career Best Finish:	26th 1996

1996 IRL PERFORMANCE PROFILE

IRL Points Championship:	30th, 9 points
IRL Best Finish:	26th, Indianapolis 500
IRL Season Earnings:	$ 153,303

27th PLACE
STEPHAN GREGOIRE

1995 REYNARD/FORD COSWORTH XB
FIRESTONE

#9 Hemelgarn Racing/Delta Faucet/Firestone
Entrant: Hemelgarn Racing, Inc.   Crew Chief: Keith Leighton

Stephan Gregoire got his best chance to return to the championship ranks with the Indy Racing League and joined Hemelgarn Racing for the inaugural season.

The young French driver had qualified seventh fastest for the 1993 Indianapolis 500 and led the race — less than a month after he saw a championship car for the first time in person. But it was his only race in the cars.

For the Indy 200 at Walt Disney World, he qualified for ninth starting spot but wound up 16th at the finish because of gearbox trouble.

In the Dura-Lube 200 at Phoenix, he started 12th and drove a steady race to seventh.

"It was difficult out there for me," Gregoire said. "It was very slippery out there today. I'm happy just to finish but I'm not proud of our performance. I was slow, but at the same time, it was a difficult race."

But it set the stage for his return to the Indianapolis Motor Speedway as a veteran. He qualified for 13th starting spot with a run of 227.556 miles per hour on Pole Day.

"I'm quite happy because yesterday, we did 222 and this morning, we came back and fixed the setup," Gregoire said. "We practiced this morning, but not a lot because there was a lot of traffic. The car was pushing and we didn't anticipate this problem, but I am very happy to be in the race."

On Race Day, he ran as high as fifth before a coil pack fire ended his day in 27th after 59 laps.

1996 INDY 500 PERFORMANCE PROFILE

Starting Position:	13
Qualifying Average:	227.556 MPH
Qualifying Speed Rank:	17
Best Practice Speed:	230.568 MPH 5/14
Total Practice Laps:	160
Number Practice Days:	5
Finishing Position:	27
Laps Completed:	59 135.068 MPH
Highest Position 1996 Race:	5
Fastest Race Lap:	47 224.355 MPH
1996 Prize Money:	$ 147,103
INDY 500 Career Earnings:	$ 336,706
Career INDY 500 Starts:	2
Career Best Finish:	19th 1993

1996 IRL PERFORMANCE PROFILE

IRL Points Championship:	10th, 165 points
IRL Best Finish:	7th, Dura-Lube 200
IRL Season Earnings:	$ 255,353

1993 LOLA/MENARD V6
FIRESTONE

JOHNNY PARSONS

#16 Team Blueprint Racing

Entrant: Team Blueprint Racing Inc.   **Crew Chief: Tom O'Brien**

Johnny Parsons saw his career at Indianapolis recharged with the newly-formed Team Blueprint and an Indy Racing League ride.

Overheating problems and contact with another car sidelined him in the Indy 200 at Walt Disney World, but the midget, sprint and Silver Crown veteran was back into championship racing.

For the Dura-Lube 200 at Phoenix, he started 17th and finished 12th when a fitting broke off the fuel pump, causing a pit fire.

At Indianapolis, he was trying to make his first "500" field since 1986 and qualified for 27th starting position on the third day of time trials at 223.843 miles per hour. It assured him of being the 34th driver to start a "500" in three different decades.

"I can't tell you how many years of heartbreak it's taken to get (back) here," Parsons said. "We're still piecing this car together and with a skeleton crew, the effort goes to them. There's nothing like being in the big show. It's great to get back to racing in the style and tradition it was meant to be."

On Race Day, trouble forced him out in 28th place after 48 laps. From 27th, he was fourth on Lap 39.

"We punctured the radiator and cooked the engine," he said. "The car really handled great. I was having a lot of fun. It's been a real roller-coaster ride. It's just good to be here."

1996 INDY 500 PERFORMANCE PROFILE

Starting Position:	27
Qualifying Average:	223.843 MPH
Qualifying Speed Rank:	28
Best Practice Speed:	224.613 MPH 5/18
Total Practice Laps:	52
Number Practice Days:	3
Finishing Position:	28
Laps Completed:	48 132.827 MPH
Highest Position 1996 Race:	4
Fastest Race Lap:	37 220.946 MPH
1996 Prize Money:	$ 161,203
INDY 500 Career Earnings:	$ 615,919
Career INDY 500 Starts:	11
Career Best Finish:	3rd 1979

1996 IRL PERFORMANCE PROFILE

IRL Points Championship:	14th, 141 points
IRL Best Finish:	12th, Dura-Lube 200
IRL Season Earnings:	$ 258,703

29th PLACE
JOHNNY
O'CONNELL

1995 REYNARD/FORD COSWORTH XB
FIRESTONE

#75 Mechanics Laundry/Cunningham Racing/Firestone
Entrant: Cunningham Racing   Crew Chief: Mark Olson

For Johnny O'Connell, the Indy Racing League was a new chapter to a racing career that had encompassed many different types of racing vehicles.

Cunningham Racing put together a yeoman effort to prepare a car for O'Connell to join the Indy 200 field and O'Connell put it in the 15th starting spot for the inaugural at Walt Disney World. He drove a steady race to seventh.

At Phoenix, before a hometown crowd, he put together another steady effort, starting 10th and finishing fifth.

At Indianapolis, he passed his driver's test only five days before the final weekend of time trials. But with one minute remaining in third-day qualifications, he became the 33rd qualifier with a four-lap average of 222.361 miles per hour.

"We were swinging at a lot of pitches and we finally hit one today," O'Connell said. "220 sounds so easy when they say it. I didn't think I'd be as jazzed as I am. Everyone pulled together and we pulled it off."

After starting 29th, he finished in the same spot after running as high as eighth, the victim of fuel pickup trouble after 47 laps.

"This is a great disappointment," O'Connell said. "This is not the way we wanted to show up and certainly not the way we wanted to finish. I started in Nebraska for all practical purposes, so it was tough."

1996 INDY 500 PERFORMANCE PROFILE

Starting Position:	29
Qualifying Average:	222.361 MPH
Qualifying Speed Rank:	32
Best Practice Speed:	225.315 MPH 5/16
Total Practice Laps:	289
Number Practice Days:	5
Finishing Position:	29
Laps Completed:	47 112.470 MPH
Highest Position 1996 Race:	8
Fastest Race Lap:	37 217.077 MPH
1996 Prize Money:	$ 145,553
INDY 500 Career Earnings:	$ 145,553
Career INDY 500 Starts:	1
Career Best Finish:	29th 1996

1996 IRL PERFORMANCE PROFILE

IRL Points Championship:	7th, 192 points
IRL Best Finish:	5th, Dura-Lube 200
IRL Season Earnings:	$ 269,303

95

1995 REYNARD/FORD COSWORTH XB
GOODYEAR

#33 Rio Hotel & Casino/Perry Ellis/Royal Purple
Entrant: Team Scandia   Crew Chief: Richie Simon

Michele Alboreto came to the United States from a distinguished Formula One career to participate in the Indy Racing League's inaugural season and almost immediately declared that it was good to be considered a "rookie" again.

After joining Team Scandia, his first experience on an oval came during winter testing at Walt Disney World and he quickly adapted.

For the Indy 200, he drove from 14th starting position to fourth at the finish.

"It's my first race (on an oval)," he said. "I'm new and I finished fourth and I'm happy."

From there, it was on to Phoenix and he again charged from the rear, going from 21st starting position to eighth.

At Indianapolis, he was a quick starter, completing the driver's test in just one hour, 41 minutes, as one of the initial group to make the grade.

After waving off on his first attempt on Pole Day, Alboreto came back to record a four-lap average of 228.229 miles per hour to gain a spot in his first Indianapolis 500.

"We had some problems on the first run because the boost was not good," he said. "We wanted to qualify the car today and we are in the top 15, so that's what's important."

He started 12th, but gearbox problems sidelined him after 43 laps. He had run as high as seventh.

1996 INDY 500 PERFORMANCE PROFILE

Starting Position:	12
Qualifying Average:	228.229 MPH
Qualifying Speed Rank:	16
Best Practice Speed:	232.192 MPH 5/14
Total Practice Laps:	389
Number Practice Days:	9
Finishing Position:	30
Laps Completed:	43 135.964 MPH
Highest Position 1996 Race:	7
Fastest Race Lap:	33 219.378 MPH
1996 Prize Money:	$ 144,953
INDY 500 Career Earnings:	$ 144,953
Career INDY 500 Starts:	1
Career Best Finish:	30th 1996

1996 IRL PERFORMANCE PROFILE

IRL Points Championship:	8th, 189 points
IRL Best Finish:	4th, Indy 200
IRL Season Earnings:	$ 283,703

31st PLACE

JOHN
PAUL, JR.

1993 LOLA/MENARD V6
GOODYEAR

#18 V-Line/Earl's Performance Products/Crowne Plaza/Keco
Entrant: PDM Racing, Inc.   Crew Chief: Chuck Buckman

John Paul Jr. became the first driver of a team formed by Paul Diatlovich and Chuck Buckman called PDM racing in time for the Indy 200 at Walt Disney World.

He qualified on his second attempt at 160.242 miles per hour and started 16th for the IRL inaugural. On Race Day, he moved up to ninth at the finish.

"I was just thrilling," Paul said. "I just wanted to finish. It's hard to believe we just started on Thursday...not much time."

It was on to Phoenix, where he qualified for 13th starting spot for the Dura-Lube 200, but engine failure sidelined him in 14th.

At Indianapolis, he waved off his first attempt on Pole Day and came back later the same day to check in at 224.757 miles per hour to gain a spot in the field.

"This morning, we went 227 in practice but then in qualifying we blew the (popoff) valve and had to reset it," Paul said. "I'm happy to be in the first day. I just would have liked to have done it the first time (in the original line)."

On Race Day, his fortunes didn't improve as ignition trouble ended his day after 10 laps in 31st position.

"The crew did a tremendous job all month," Paul said. "This is very disappointing. The engine had a misfire in it from the start. We thought we had a good package for today...too bad we didn't get to show it."

1996 INDY 500 PERFORMANCE PROFILE

Starting Position:	17
Qualifying Average:	224.757 MPH
Qualifying Speed Rank:	25
Best Practice Speed:	227.192 MPH 5/11
Total Practice Laps:	200
Number Practice Days:	8
Finishing Position:	31
Laps Completed:	10 81.140 MPH
Highest Position 1996 Race:	19
Fastest Race Lap:	6 193.137 MPH
1996 Prize Money:	$ 144,203
INDY 500 Career Earnings:	$ 793,422
Career INDY 500 Starts:	5
Career Best Finish:	10th 1992

1996 IRL PERFORMANCE PROFILE

IRL Points Championship:	12th 153 points
IRL Best Finish:	9
IRL Season Earnings:	$ 249,953

1992 LOLA/BUICK
GOODYEAR

#96 ABF Motorsports USA/Sunrise Rental Canada
Entrant: ABF Motorsports LLC   Crew Chief: Darrell Soppe

Paul Durant was the first to exceed 150 miles an hour in a supermodified at Phoenix International Raceway's one-mile oval and his first ride in a championship car came at the Dura-Lube 200 on the same track.

He completed his driver's test on Friday of race weekend in an ABF Motorsports entry.

"The Indy cars and supermodifieds are very similar," Durant said. "The corner speeds are much greater in the Indy cars but there really is no big difference with the horsepower."

His debut was short-lived as front-end problems ended his day after one lap in 22nd place.

On Day 4 of practice for the Indianapolis 500, he became the 13th to pass the driver's test. He qualified on the second day of time trials with a four-lap average of 225.404 miles per hour.

"The car was still tight," Durant said. "We made a couple of radical changes but they didn't make much of a difference. We would have liked a 227, but the goal was to go over 225 and qualify fast enough to make the field."

On Race Day, engine failure sent him to the sidelines after nine laps and he finished 32nd.

"The motor let go," he said. "It was in a good spot because I thought I could try to get it down to the warmup lane. I guess I got in my own oil and it got around on me. I got on the brakes as fast as I could. The main thing is, we didn't get in anyone else's way."

1996 INDY 500 PERFORMANCE PROFILE

Starting Position:	24
Qualifying Average:	225.404 MPH
Qualifying Speed Rank:	24
Best Practice Speed:	226.165 MPH 5/12
Total Practice Laps:	176
Number Practice Days:	6
Finishing Position:	32
Laps Completed:	9 137.701 MPH
Highest Position 1996 Race:	19
Fastest Race Lap:	9 200.410 MPH
1996 Prize Money:	$ 149,153
INDY 500 Career Earnings:	$ 149,153
Career INDY 500 Starts:	1
Career Best Finish:	32th 1996

1996 IRL PERFORMANCE PROFILE

IRL Points Championship:	22nd, 32 points
IRL Best Finish:	22nd, Dura-Lube 200
IRL Season Earnings:	$ 159,153

33rd PLACE
JOHNNY UNSER

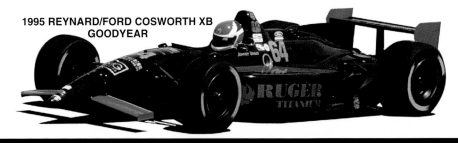

1995 REYNARD/FORD COSWORTH XB
GOODYEAR

#64 Ruger-Titanium/Project Indy/Reynard
Entrant: Project Indy   Crew Chief: Dave Dras

Johnny Unser joined the long list of members of the Unser family in making his way in the field for the Indianapolis 500.

He got his Indy Racing League start at Phoenix, where he joined the Project Indy team for the Dura-Lube 200.

He passed his refresher test and qualified 19th. From there, he drove a steady race to finish ninth, running at the end.

It was on to Indianapolis, where he became the 12th driver of the month to pass his driver's test, making the grade on Day 4.

On Pole Day, he registered a four-lap run averaging 226.115 miles per hour. In doing so, he became the first rookie to "lock in" a spot in the field at the age of 37.

"Me being the only Unser here I thought would never happen," he said. "We were real close to being here last year. This is the '500.' This is the greatest race in the world. Being able to come here is very special. We had a good solid car. All four laps were smooth. I'm pleased with it for the time we had."

On Race Day, though, trouble struck early, and Unser pulled to pit road at the end of the parade lap. His day ended before the green flag fell and he was awarded 33rd finishing position.

"The gearbox just broke," Unser said. "I don't know why yet but I couldn't get it in gear. It was a disappointing day for all of us."

1996 INDY 500 PERFORMANCE PROFILE

Starting Position:	16
Qualifying Average:	226.115 MPH
Qualifying Speed Rank:	22
Best Practice Speed:	227.238 MPH 5/11
Total Practice Laps:	354
Number Practice Days:	10
Finishing Position:	33
Laps Completed:	0
Highest Position 1996 Race:	33
Fastest Race Lap:	0
1996 Prize Money:	$ 143,953
INDY 500 Career Earnings:	$ 143,953
Career INDY 500 Starts:	1
Career Best Finish:	33rd 1996

1996 IRL PERFORMANCE PROFILE

IRL Points Championship:	19th, 56 points
IRL Best Finish:	9th, Dura-Lube 200
IRL Season Earnings:	$ 188,203

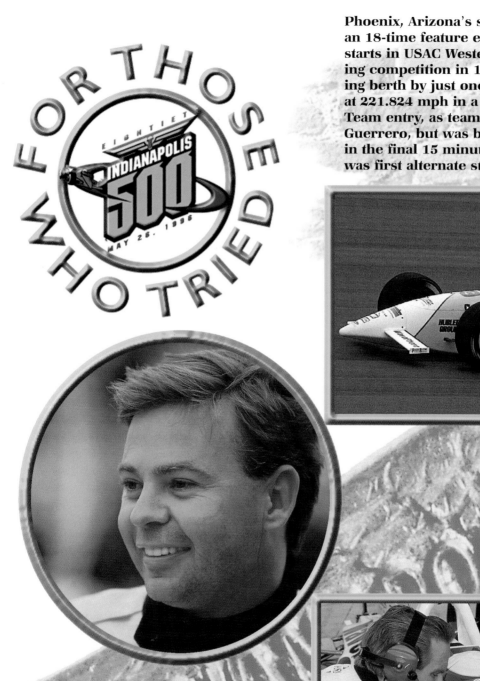

FOR THOSE WHO TRIED

Phoenix, Arizona's sensational Billy Boat, an 18-time feature event winner out of 27 starts in USAC Western States midget racing competition in 1995, missed a 500 starting berth by just one position. He qualified at 221.824 mph in a second Pagan Racing Team entry, as teammate to Roberto Guerrero, but was bumped from the field in the final 15 minutes of time trials and was first alternate starter for the race.

After passing his rookie test in Loop Hole Racing Team's #36, Tyce Carlson took over the Brickell Racing Group's #77 at the last minute and almost made the starting field. His four-lap average speed of 221.201 mph, just as the time trials were ending, was not quite fast enough to get in.

New Zealand-born Rob Wilson ran over 650 miles of practice in Project Indy's #46 but did not make a qualifying attempt.

FOR THOSE WHO TRIED

EIGHTIETH INDIANAPOLIS 500 MAY 26, 1996

The high aspirations of Idaho's Randy Tolsma came to an end when his McCormack Motorsports #24 spun into the outer retaining wall on the afternoon of the final qualifying day.

102

Dan Drinan (top) and Andy Michner (right) both passed their rookie test in Loop Hole Racing Teams #36 as did Tyce Carlson. Drinan had an accident with the car while trying to build to qualifying speed.

The Tempero-Giuffre team practiced with two cars, #15 and #25, but neither Joe Gosek, who later qualified for another team, or England's Justin Bell (pictured here) could get them up to speed. Justin is the son of many-time LeMans 24-Hours race winner Derek Bell.

EPILOGUE

By Jan Shaffer

The 80th month of May was different, because it took on a personality all its own.

The loss of Scott Brayton was incalculable in the equation. The popular veteran, known for his enthusiasm and vigor, was more than a race driver. He was a friend to so many for so long at the Speedway that he became a symbol of what the Indianapolis 500 meant to fans and aspiring drivers alike.

His passing came after his own highest of highs. Scott Brayton will be remembered by us all for his humor and energy. He will also be in the history books as well, as the driver sent to the line by John Menard and Larry Curry to bring back the pole for the 80th Indianapolis 500 on one of the most dramatic qualifying days in Speedway lore.

As a person, Scotty was a fine friend, husband and father. As a race driver, he will forever hold a significant place in the legend of the "500."

But there were positive feelings to the month of May, aspects which Brayton embraced and typified by his bright, enthusiastic style.

A racing family came together in more ways than one during the Indy Racing League's first season. Crews in Gasoline Alley helped each other. Veteran drivers helped newcomers learn the ways of the Speedway, on and off the track. There was a warm, genuine spirit of cooperation. There were dreams and goals.

Felicia McCormack, co-owner of McCormack Motorsports with her husband, Dennis, stopped by the press room early in the month.

"It's different this year," she remarked at the time. "People walk in, smile, say hello and it's a great atmosphere all around. We haven't had this much fun since the garage doors were green."

Lee Kunzman, team manager for Hemelgarn Racing, told the story about the new driver who stopped by the Hemelgarn garage for a chat.

"He said, 'Now my career is complete. If I don't drive another race car again, I've driven one around the Indianapolis Motor Speedway,'" Kunzman related. "I thought about that and it caused me to remember why I've been coming here for the past 25 years. It turned the light on."

After the race, there was concern and a long recovery road ahead for veteran Alessandro Zampedri, who suffered serious leg, ankle and foot injuries in the last-lap accident.

After multiple surgeries and therapy, Zampedri was on crutches by October and well on his way back.

"My right foot is completely healed," Zampedri said in the fall. "We're now in the phase of optimizing it. My left foot is doing well, too. We have to wait until the bone graft is completely healed, but I'm walking with 30 pounds on it now. I'm walking 20 minutes every day. It's quite a challenge if you haven't done it for so long.

"Looking at my history of how I've been healing, I'm hoping to walk probably for Christmas. It's an optimistic goal...maybe with a cane."

He hopes to return to the cockpit in time for the 1997 Indianapolis 500.

"Yes, indeed," he said. "That's what I want to do. I believe, if it does or doesn't happen, it's not going to be from my physical condition.

"It's very important to me for many different reasons. The first month, month-and-a-half, I wasn't thinking anything at all. In another phase, I started thinking a little bit, then I decided I want to do it again. (To do it), it has to be worth it. I have to have a chance to win. I basically left Indy with the lead with 11 laps to go.

Now I proved I can be at the top, can lead the race. I'm just hoping I can take it from there and go to Victory Lane.

"The '500' meant a lot to me as a race-car driver. It gave me so much more popularity. It built up my name and reputation like nothing ever did before — in the United States, but mostly in my home country of Italy. It's the greatest race in the world. Being here, being in the race is just incredible."

SPONSORS

OFFICIAL PACE CAR

True Value
OFFICIAL HARDWARE STORE

OFFICIAL MOTOR OIL

OFFICIAL TRAILER

ACDelco

BOSCH

CHAMPION

OFFICIAL SPONSORS

RAYBESTOS "TOP FINISHING ROOKIE" AWARD
$10,000 - Raybestos
Buzz Calkins

TRUE VALUE "MASTER MECHANIC" AWARD
(pole winning chief mechanic)
$10,000 - Cotter & Company
Brian Nott (Buddy Lazier)

MILLER ELECTRIC "HARD CHARGER" AWARD
(lowest qualifier to lead the race)
$5,000 - Miller Electric
Robbie Buhl

VALVOLINE "MECHANIC OF THE RACE" AWARD
$5,000 - Valvoline, Inc.
Chris Beck (Robbie Buhl)

AMERICAN DAIRY "FASTEST ROOKIE" AWARD
(fastest qualifying rookie)
$2,500 - American Dairy Association
Richie Hearn

CHAMPION SPARK PLUG
$10,000

DELCO BATTERY
$10,000

VALVOLINE, INC.
$7,500

STP PRODUCTS
$8,000

EARL'S PERFORMANCE PRODUCTS
$7,500

ROBERT BOSCH CORP.
$2,000

EMCO GEARS, INC.
$1,000

RAYBESTOS "TOP FINISHING ROOKIE" AWARD
$10,000 - Raybestos
Richie Hearn

TRUE VALUE "MASTER MECHANIC" AWARD
(pole winning chief mechanic)
$10,000 - Cotter & Company
Brad McCanless (Arie Luyendyk)

AMERICAN DAIRY "FASTEST ROOKIE" AWARD
(fastest qualifying rookie)
$2,500 - American Dairy Association
Richie Hearn

CHAMPION SPARK PLUG
$10,000

DELCO BATTERY
$10,000

EARL'S PERFORMANCE PRODUCTS
$7,500

J.C. CARTER
$7,500

STP PRODUCTS
$6,000

ROBERT BOSCH CORP.
$2,000

EMCO GEARS, INC.
$1,000

CONTINGENCY AWARDS

AMERICAN YARD PRODUCTS
$5,000

BELL HELMETS
$6,000

CANON, U.S.A
$12,000

CHAMPION SPARK PLUG
$40,000

DELPHI AUTOMOTIVE SYSTEMS
$25,000

EARL'S PERFORMANCE PRODUCTS
$20,000

EMCO GEARS, INC.
$5,000

FIRST BRANDS STP RACING
$26,000

HYPERCO INC.
$5,000

IDEAL DIVISION STANT CORP.
$5,000

J.C. CARTER COMPANY, INC.
$7,500

LOCTITE CORPORATION
$9,500

MALLORY INC.
$5,000

MOBIL OIL CORPORATION
$5,000

MONROE AUTO EQUIPMENT
$20,000

PPG INDUSTRIES, INC.
$495,000

PENNZOIL PRODUCTS COMPANY
$13,000

PREMIER INDUSTRIAL CORPORATION
$10,000

QUAKER STATE CORPORATION
$25,000

RAYBESTOS/BRAKE PARTS INC.
$30,000

ROBERT BOSCH CORPORATION
$45,000

SIMPSON RACE PRODUCTS
$10,000

SNAP-ON TOOLS CORP.
$5,000

STANT MANUFACTURING, INC.
$5,000

VALVOLINE, INC.
$50,000

PPG Pole Award $100,000
PPG INDUSTRIES
Plus a 1996 customized Dodge/Tiara van ($35,000 value)
DODGE and TIARA MOTORCOACH CORPORATION
Scott Brayton

GTE "Front Runner" Award - $30,000
$10,000 awarded to each front row driver
GTE
Scott Brayton, Tony Stewart, Davy Jones

True Value "Pole Winning Chief Mechanic" Award - $10,000
COTTER AND COMPANY
Kevin Blanch

Sure Start/Automotive Armature "On The Bubble" Award - $10,000
awarded to the 33rd fastest qualifier
EXIDE CORPORATION
Scott Harrington

Ameritech "Youngest Starting Driver" Award - $7,500
AMERITECH
Michel Jourdain Jr.

Tiara "Pole Position Car Owner" Award - $5,000
TIARA MOTORCOACH CORPORATION
John Menard

Kruse International "First in the Field" Award - $5,000
KRUSE INTERNATIONAL
Lyn St. James

American Dairy "Fastest Qualifying Rookie" Award - $5,000
AMERICAN DAIRY ASSOCIATION
Tony Stewart

Pinkerton Security "Most Senior Starting Driver" Award - $5,000
PINKERTON SECURITY & INVESTIGATION
Lyn St. James

Delco Battery/CAM "Great Start" Award - $5,000
awarded to the chief mechanic of the team which records the most first-week practice laps and qualifies on Pole Day
AC DELCO/CHAMPIONSHIP ASSOCIATION OF MECHANICS, INC.
Jack Pegues (Alessandro Zampedri)

Buckeye Machine/Race Spec "Final Measure" Award - $5,000
awarded to last team to pass inspection and qualify for the race
BUCKEYE MACHINE/RACE SPEC
Joe Gosek

T.P. Donovan "Top Starting Rookie" Award - $5,000
OLINGER DISTRIBUTING COMPANY, INC.
Tony Stewart

S R E Industries "My Bubble Burst" Award - $5,000
awarded to the last driver to be bumped on last day of qualifying
SRE INDUSTRIES
Billy Boat

NewsPager "Most Consistent Qualifying Laps" Award - $5,000
NEWSPAGER MOTORSPORTS
Tony Stewart

Snap-On Tools/CAM "500 Top Wrench" Award - $5,000
awarded to the chief mechanic demonstrating outstanding skill and expertise during qualifying
SNAP-ON TOOLS/CHAMPIONSHIP ASSOCIATION OF MECHANICS, INC.
Kevin Blanch

The Marmon Group "Fastest Rookie Lap" Award - $5,000
THE MARMON GROUP
Tony Stewart

Citadel Group "Overachiever" Award - $5,000
awarded to the team who achieves the greatest qualifying success with limited resources
CITADEL GROUP
Paul Durant

Mi-Jack "Top Performance" Award - $5,000
awarded to the driver recording the fastest single qualifying lap
MI-JACK PRODUCTS
Arie Luyendyk

Nissan "Rookie Owner" Award - $5,000
awarded to the highest qualifying rookie team owner
NISSAN MOTOR CORPORATION
Brad Calkins, Bradley Motorsports

Loctite "Permatex Fast Orange" Award - $5,000
awarded to the pole position winner
LOCTITE CORPORATION
Scott Brayton

BORG-WARNER TROPHY AWARD
$130,000 plus trophy replica - Borg-Warner Automotive, Inc.
Buddy Lazier

DODGE OFFICIAL PACE CAR AWARD
1996 Dodge Viper GTS Official Pace Car - Dodge
Buddy Lazier

COORS PIT STOP CHALLENGE
$51,000 - Coors Brewing Company *(contest held May 23, 1996)*
Davy Jones

DOW ELANCO "MILESTONE" AWARDS
$25,000 - DowElanco *(race leaders at 100, 200, 300 and 400 miles)*
Buddy Lazier (100 miles), Davy Jones (200, 300 and 400 miles)

AMERICAN DAIRY AWARDS
$10,750 - American Dairy Association
(winner, fastest rookie, winning chief mechanic)
Buddy Lazier, Tony Stewart, Brian Nott

LOCTITE AWARDS
$10,500 - Loctite Corporation and Permatex Fast Orange
(winner, winning chief mechanic, pole position)
Buddy Lazier, Brian Nott, Scott Brayton

BANK ONE "ROOKIE OF THE YEAR" AWARD
$10,000 - Bank One, Indianapolis
Tony Stewart

IBM "FASTEST LAP" AWARD
$10,000 - IBM Corporation *(fastest single lap of the race)*
Eddie Cheever

KODAK "PHOTO FINISH" AWARD
$10,000 - Eastman Kodak Company *(race winner)*
Buddy Lazier

NBD "LEADERS' CIRCLE" AWARD
$10,000 - NBD Bank
(awarded to the driver who leads the most laps in the race)
Roberto Guerrero

NATIONAL CITY BANK "CHECKERED FLAG" AWARD
$10,000 - National City Bank, Indiana *(race winner)*
Buddy Lazier

CHAPMAN S. ROOT AWARD
$5,000 - Terre Haute First National Bank *(race leader at lap 48)*
Tony Stewart

CLINT BRAWNER "MECHANICAL EXCELLENCE" AWARD
$5,000 - Clint Brawner Mechanical Excellence Award Foundation
Johnny Parsons

GOODYEAR "WINNING CAR OWNER" AWARD
$5,000 plus ring - The Goodyear Tire and Rubber Co.
Ron Hemelgarn

INDIANA OXYGEN "PERSEVERANCE" AWARD
$5,000 - Indiana Oxygen
*(team who exemplifies the most exceptional
sportsmanship in a non-winning effort)*
Arie Luyendyk

MARSH "LEADER AT LAP 65" AWARD
$5,000 - Marsh Supermarkets, Inc.
(race leader at lap 3)
Roberto Guerrero

MILLER ELECTRIC "HARD CHARGER" AWARD
$5,000 - Miller Electric
(lowest qualifier to lead the race)
Alessandro Zampedri

MOTORSPORTS SPARES/GOODRIDGE "PERSISTENCE PAYS" AWARD
$5,000 - Motorsports Spares Int'l Inc./ Goodridge
(highest finishing last day qualifier)
Hideshi Matsuda

PREMIER/D-A "MECHANICAL ACHIEVEMENT" AWARD
$5,000 - Premier Industrial Corp.
Team Menard

KLIPSCH/OVERHEAD DOOR "EFFICIENCY" AWARD
$5,000 - Klipsch, Inc./Overhead Door Company
(awarded to the team that runs the most miles between pit stops)
Hideshi Matsuda

NISSAN "ROOKIE OWNER" AWARD
$5,000 - Nissan Motor Corporation USA
(awarded to the highest finishing rookie team owner)
John Della Penna

PENNZOIL PERFORMAX® 100 "Performance" Award
$5,000 - Pennzoil Products Company
(winning chief mechanic)
Brian Nott

"STIHL THE LEADER" AWARD
$5,000 - Stihl, Inc.
(awarded to the team on the leading edge of technology)
Bradley Motorsports (Buzz Calkins)

SUN INDUSTRIES "COMPETITIVE SPIRIT" AWARD
$5,000 - Sun Industries
(awarded to the lowest position car still running at the finish)
Marco Greco

SYSCO "SOARING TO SUCCESS" AWARD
$5,000 - SYSCO
(race winner)
Buddy Lazier

THUNDERBIRD "WINNER'S" AWARD
$5,000 plus a Formula 271-SR-1 boat - Thunderbird Products
(race winner)
Buddy Lazier

TRUCKERS TOY STORE "RACE TRANSPORTER" AWARD
$5,000 - Truckers Toy Store, Inc.
(best tractor, trailer and tractor/trailer combination)
AJ Foyt Enterprises, Team Menard, Team Scandia

Robert G. Moorhead, Chairman of the Board; Thomas W. Binford, Vice-Chairman of the Board; Richard King, President; Henry C. Ryder, Secretary; Arthur A. Angotti, Treasurer; Johnny Capels, Executive Vice President/ Competition Director; Cary Agajanian, Executive Vice-President/IRL; Robert Cassaday, Vice President/Administration; Michael Devin, Vice President/Technical Director; Art Graham, Vice President/ Development; Bill Marvel, Vice President/Corporate Affairs; Gary Sokola, Deputy Competition Director; Tommy Hunt, Vice President/Western States Operations; Ray Linton, Vice President/Finance; Dick Jordan, Communications Director.

EXECUTIVE OFFICIALS

Keith D. Ward, Chief Steward; Arthur D. Meyers, Senior Steward; Robert Cassaday, Steward/Chief Registrar; Rich Coy, Steward; John Notte III, Steward; Michael Devin, Technical Director; Art Graham, Director of Timing & Scoring.

STARTERS

Duane Sweeney, Chief Starter; Ray Chaike, Brian Howard, Assistant Starters.

OBSERVERS

Claude Fisher, Chief Observer; Edwin Board, Mike Lake, Ted Lake and Robert Stanley, Deputy Chief Observers; Dennis Barker, Jeff Boles, Butch Bundrant, Gary Goodrich, Denis Goonen, Jim Haynes, Richard Hoehnke, Pat Johnson, Robert Ledbetter, Robert Maas, Philip Manuel and Glenn Timmis, Assistant Chief Observers.

Observers: S.Amos, J.Bailey, A.Barker, R.J.Barron, R.N.Barron, D.Barth, M.Bennett, N.Bennett, W.Borecki, J.Boucher, J.Brasker, R.Brown, F.Bruckner, G.Bundrant, J.Butler, R.Clark, W.Clark, M.L. Coble, R.J. Coble, M.Cox, R.Cox, Jr., S.Cox, R.Cross, D.Crouch, L.Crouch, L.Davis, V.Dentice, D.Distler, J.Dudley, G.Edwards, L.Ellis, D.Emerick, F.Frost, N.Giordano, D.Goonen, R.Hamilton, T.Hare, J.Highsmith, K.Hoffman, R.Hogan, L.Hough, G.Humphrey, C.Hurt, L.Hurt, D.Konkler, L.Kunkle, F.Kurtz, D.Lanham, S.Lawson, L.Leser, D.Lindsey, W.Loucks, M.Lykins, T.Martin, C.McGuire, G.Parsons, J.Payne, R.Peterson, C.Pierson, D.Price, M.Reinking, J.Schaffner, G.Schultz, Scott Schultz, Steve Schultz, B.Sewell, J.Simko, G.Snider, J.Snider, T.Stawicki, R.Stoddard, J.Stubblefield, R.Sumner, G.Sweeney, L.Sweeney, S.Taylor, D.Thompson, J.Tillett, J.Topp, T.Totura, N.Trebing, R.Vannice, J.Walden, G.Werner, S.West, P.Whalen, P.J.Whalen, V.Whorton, G.Wirey, E.Wright, T.Wyn, Observers.

MISCELLANEOUS

Supervisor of Track Fire Prevention - Jack Gilmore; Score Board Manager - David Adams; Chief Announcer - Tom Carnegie; Telephone Service - Indiana Bell Co. and AT&T; Wrecker Service - No*Mar Towing Equipment; and Welding Service - Indiana Oxygen Company.

TECHNICAL OPERATIONS

Michael Devin, Technical Director; Mark Bridges, Deputy Director; Jerry Grobe, Assistant Deputy Director; Dennis Hunley, Assistant Director NDT & Metallurgical Committee; D. Ray Marshall, Assistant Director, Race-Spec; Jack Beckley, Donald McGregor, Technical Advisors; Samuel Burge, Ray Linton, Ron Scudder and Mike Smith, Supervisors; Andy Anderson, Anne Grobe, John W. Grobe, Jack Jenkins, Steve Jordan, David Kyle, Ray Macht, Pat Martin, Jerry Smith, Kevin Smith, Russ Stone, Terry Taylor, William Teeguarden, Jeff VanTreese and Jon VanTreese, Vice Chairmen; Roam Jordan, Marcel Periat and William Sparks, Advisors at Large.

TECHNICAL ASSISTANTS

Dennis Brankle, Gary Brewer, Lila Brewer, Barry Cole, Debbie Collins, Jeff Collins, Pam Dooley, Bud Edwards, Cathy Hoy, Rick Hoy, Candee Mackell, Joseph Mackell, Nancy Marshall, Wayne Messenger, Penny Meyers, Tom Miller, Rick Myers, Kevin Park, Linda Park, Paul Park, Sandy Park, Steve Park, Paul Powers, Mike Reffitt, John Shark, Dave Simpson, Larry Stubbs, Dennis Thacker and Jill Thacker, Race Spec Inspection; E.Budy, Jr., B.Collins, J.Cullen, J.Eifert, J.Freeze, L.Haynes, J. Hunley, S.Hunley, D.Janos, D.Jenkins, C.Kiracofe, J.Knavel, S.Kontney, T.L.Kontney, C.Majors, B.Messer, M.Miener, T.Miller, B.Newkirk, H.Ray, H.Rohm, Jr., N.Rufinio, D.Shelton, C.Small, L.Snyder, M.Sullivan, W.Tarpley, D.Taylor, C.Trotter, A.Valvo, L.Vaniwarden, and M.Zink, Non-Destructive Testing; Dave King, Communications; Harry Robertson, Fuel Cell Advisor; Terry Haley, Assistant Weigh Master; Paige Green, Sandy Griffith, Pat McCarty, Martha Shields, Toni Sylvester and Susan Vigil, Technical Data; A.Adastik, A.Albrecht, D.Anderson, A.Ankerman, P.Asa, H.Baker, J.Baker, R.Banks, D.Barrett, S.Bell, A.Biggs, R.Bivens, G.Bloeser, J.Bornhorst, W.Brizius, D.Bullock, F.Burdette, R.Butterfield, P.Cannaley, R.Carpenter, R.Carson, J.Clark, V.Clossin, B.Clough, F.Collins, K.Collins, R.Cooper, J.Cowley, D.Cox, E.Cox, C.Curry, S.Detrick, S.Dorazio, W.Dunkerson, D.Dunning, B.Edwards, T.Edwards, M.Ehnert, R.Elsner, B.Eves, B.Fahey, R.Falcon, C.Fielder, T.Finney, C.Fischer, G.Frashier, B.Gammon, J.M.Grobe, R.Grobe, R.Hanson, C.Harmon, C.Hartzer, E.Held, D.Herling, J.Innis, J.Jenkins, D.Johansen, J.Johnson, S.Kelly, K.Korhonen, K.Krimmel, E.Labiak, J.Lautenschlager, B.Leatherman, H.Lemcool, S.Lewis, D.Love, J.Maher, T.Martin, J.Mastin, J.Mayhew, H.Merritt, M.Milharcik, R.Murphy, J.Nell, J.Nims, C.Parmelli, S.Pelsor, A.Pickett, M.Ray, J.Rayhel, T.Reed, R.Riffel, A.Schmidt, M.Selode, N.Shields, B.Smith, J.Smith, F.Snow, R.Stern, W.Strong, B.Turner, R.VanNote, D.Verrill, A.Vesely, A.Vesely, Jr., C.Wasdyke, C.Wasdyke, Jr., P.Wilson, G.Yohe, Technical Observers. Certification Committee: Jack Stamper, Chairman; Carl Colip, William Conley, Walter Kuhn, Frank Wilhelm, Deputy Directors; D.Cherry, R.Condit, C.Einspahr, D.Gunder, S.Ingle, K.Kapitan, D.Kischell, S.Lanham, J.Locke, G.Mayfield, D.Nicely, J.Proper, D.Smith, Vice Chairmen.

SAFETY OFFICIALS

Jack Gilmore, Director; Robert Nolen, Deputy Director.

TIMING & SCORING

Art Graham, Director: Les Kimbrell, Director of Scoring Operations; Barbara Hellyer, Deputy Director -Scoring Systems; Chuck Whetsel, Deputy Director - Timing Systems; Larry Allen, Chief Scoring Technician; Jerry L. Challis, Chief Scorer; Mike Cramer, Chief Scoring Registrar; Dennis Dyer, Senior Scoring Engineer; Andrew Graham, Chief of Scoring Systems; Harold Hamilton, Chief Timing Engineer; Kay Kimbrell, Chief Serial Scorer; Larry Martin, Chief Scoring Engineer; Jack Taylor, Chief Scoring Observer; George Vogelsperger, Chief Pit Scorer; Dick Webb, Chief Auditor; Bert Wilkerson, Chief of Scoring Equipment; Ray Szeluga, Honorary Chief Scorer; Mile Wiley, Honorary Chief Scorer.

Timing & Scoring Staff: Larry Albean, John Alexander, Bill Ballard Jr., Dave Berryman, Andy Blahut, Bob Blahut, Bruce Boyd, Connie Brethman, Barbara Bucher, Joyce Diemer, Patrick Diemer, Linda Foster, Veronica Frost, D.J.áGarrison, Michael Gray, Ed Harvey, Ryan Hoover, Lisa Lengerich, Ed Long, Jim Macino, Ken Mallette, Dawn Moss, Craig Newman, Gary Paschke, Larry Potter, George Radziwill, Kent Rebman, Nick Reed, Bill Reeser, Dale Smiley, Bill Spellerberg, Bill Stevens, Don Stone, Craig Wambold, Bert Wilkerson II, Don Wilkerson, Terry Wilkerson, Chuck Yoder.

Technical Partners Staff: Dave Moore, Dave McCarter (IBM Corp.); Scooter Willis, Kent Tambling (Digital Solutions); Ray Szeluga (Lexmark Corp.).

Additional Race Day Personnel: J.Akers, M.Albean, B.Alexander, B.Armbruster, S.Arnold, L.Ashburn, J.Baden, B.BallardáIII, J.Bertholf, S.Blank, R.Bromwell, B.Campbell, D.Campbell, D.Challis, B.Cole, S.E-Coles, W.Coles, J.Compton, L.Crane, S.Crane, S.Demeter, C.Derbin, M.Ellis, J.Engledow, R.Fegan, N.Funkhouser, B.Gardner, D.Gentry, D.Graham, D.Gramlik, S.Gray, S.Griffith, R.Hanes, G.Harabin, L.Harabin, R.Harvey, N.Hastings, B.Hicks, D.Hindman, S.Holt Jr., Randy Hoover, S.Hoover, B.Hunter, D.Hunter, S.Hunter, A.Irons, P.Karle, R.Kenyon, J.Lane, E.Leduke, B.Lindholm, C.Macomber, T.McKinney, L.Mitchell, B.Mooney, B.Moore, H.Moore, S.Moore, C.Moorman, J.Morphy, B.Mount, B.Moyer, A.Neuner, S.Oliver, L.Olson, J.Paschke, K.Paschke, Jeff Perkins, Jim Perkins, John Perkins, J.Pingle, D.Renzoni, R.Renzoni, B.Reynolds, D.Richey, E.Rodman, D.Rutledge, C.Schendel, J.Schuh, M.Sedam, C.Serafin, G.Simpson, S.Steele, R.Stone, C.Tunny, Greg Vogelsperger, P.Voorhees, S.Voorhees, B.Weir, S.Wright, J.Youngblood.

Trackside Computing by the IBM PC with OS/2, the Information Systems Choice of the United States Auto Club Support Services courtesy of IBM INDIANA

MEDICAL STAFF & SUPPORT

Administrative Staff: Medical Director, Henry C. Bock, M.D.; Assistant Medical Director, Michael L. Olinger, M.D.; Medical Administrator, Cheryl Rumer, R.N.; Nursing Director, Therese Cordell, R.N.; Optometrist, E. Jerome Babitz, O.D.; EMS Coordinator, Andrew Bowes, EMT-P; Executive Secretary, Mary Simpson.

CHAPLAINS

Reverend Michael Welch and Dr. Andrew Crowley.

1996 IRL DRIVER POINT STANDINGS

	Driver	No. of Starts	Running of Finish	Highest Finish	Laps Led	Laps Completed	Total Points	Total Prize Winnings
1	Buzz Calkins	3	2	1	130	541	246	$376,553
1	Scott Sharp	3	1	2	40	578	246	361,303
3	Robbie Buhl	3	2	3	21	543	240	351,153
4	Richie Hearn	3	2	3	7	415	237	512,203
5	Roberto Guerrero	3	1	5	47	484	237	439,503
6	Mike Groff	3	2	3	0	516	228	306,253
7	Arie Luyendyk	3	1	1	122	481	225	414,003
8	Tony Stewart	3	1	2	82	447	204	375,303
9	Davey Hamilton	3	1	12	2	431	192	286,503
10	Johnny O Connell	3	2	5	0	439	192	269,303
11	Michele Alboreto	3	2	4	0	428	189	283,703
12	Lyn St. James	3	1	8	0	356	186	264,853
13	Stephan Gregoire	3	1	7	0	318	165	255,353
14	Buddy Lazier	2	1	1	71	261	159	1,446,854
15	John Paul, Jr.	3	1	9	0	316	153	249,953
16	Eddie Cheever	2	1	10	0	373	147	281,353
17	Johnny Parsons	3	0	12	0	242	141	258,703
18	Scott Brayton	2	0	15	0	175	111	235,000
19	Dave Kudrave	2	0	10	0	172	80	99,250
20	Michel Jourdain, Jr.	2	1	13	0	208	74	247,403
21	Jim Guthrie	2	0	15	0	259	74	206,453
22	Fermin Velez	2	0	19	0	139	60	210,653
23	Eliseo Salazar	1	0	6	0	197	58	236,653
24	Johnny Unser	2	1	9	0	185	56	188,203
25	Stan Wattles	1	0	13	2	144	44	50,000
26	Davy Jones	1	1	2	46	200	33	632,503
27	Paul Durant	2	0	22	0	10	32	159,153
28	Alessandro Zampedri	1	0	4	20	199	31	270,853
29	Danny Ongais	1	1	7	0	197	28	228,253
30	Hideshi Matsuda	1	1	8	0	197	27	233,953
31	Scott Harrington	1	0	15	0	150	20	190,753
32	Racin Gardner	1	0	25	0	76	20	149,853
33	Mark Dismore	1	0	19	0	129	16	161,253
34	Joe Gosek	1	0	22	0	106	13	169,653
35	Brad Murphey	1	0	23	0	91	12	177,853
36	Marco Greco	1	0	26	0	64	9	153,303
37	Dan Drinan	0	0	0	0	0	0	5,000
38	Billy Boat	0	0	0	0	0	0	5,000
39	Butch Brickell	0	0	0	0	0	0	5,000
40	Jim Buick	0	0	0	0	0	0	5,000
41	Bill Tempero	0	0	0	0	0	0	10,000
42	Rick DeLorto	0	0	0	0	0	0	10,000

Total   **$10,773,600**

STARTING LINEUP
INDY 200 AT
WALT DISNEY WORLD
JANUARY 27, 1996

	CAR		DRIVER	CAR NAME	YR/C/E/T	TIME	SPEED
1	91		Buddy Lazier	Hemelgarn Racing/Delta Faucet	95/R/F/F	19.847	181.388
2	21		Roberto Guerrero	WavePhore/Johnny Lightning	94/R/F/G	20.210	178.130
3	35		Arie Luyendyk	Jonathan Byrd's Cafeteria/Bryant Heating & Cooling	95/R/F/G	20.305	177.296
4	41		Scott Sharp	AJ Foyt Enterprises	95/L/F/G	20.430	176.211
5	12	R	Buzz Calkins	Bradley Foodmart/Total Petroleum/MBNA/Logo Athletic	95/R/F/F	20.517	175.464
6	14	R	Davey Hamilton	AJ Foyt Enterprises	95/L/F/G	20.537	175.293
7	20	R	Tony Stewart	Quaker State/Glidden	95/L/M/G	20.624	174.554
8	17	R	Stan Wattles	Leigh Miller Racing Car	94/L/F/F	20.752	173.477
9	9		Stephan Gregoire	Pierre Qui Mousse/SG Motorsports	95/R/F/F	20.780	173.244
10	2		Scott Brayton	Glidden	95/L/M/G	20.787	173.185
11	90		Lyn St. James	Lifetime Channel/Maxlube/Lola Ford Cosworth	94/L/F/G	21.039	171.111
12	11		Mike Groff	AJ Foyt Enterprises	95/L/F/G	21.095	170.657
13	54	R	Robbie Buhl	Beck Motorsports/Zunne Group/Safety-Kleen	94/R/F/F	21.107	170.560
14	33	R	Michele Alboreto	Alta-Fresh Spring Water/Perry Ellis/Lola Ford Cosworth	95/L/F/G	21.121	170.446
15	75	R	Johnny O'Connell	Ultimate Energy/Optima Batteries/MBNA	95/R/F/F	21.462	167.738
16	18		John Paul, Jr.	PDM/Automatic Sprinkler Systems	93/L/F/G	22.466	160.242
17	16		Johnny Parsons	Linkite/Firestone	93/L/M/F	23.451	153.512
18	25		Dave Kudrave	D.A.R.E./BodyLines	92/L/B/G	24.598	146.353
19	34	R	Richie Hearn	Ralph's-Food 4 Less/Della Penna Motorsports	95/R/F/G	19.900	180.905
20	3		Eddie Cheever	Quaker State	95/L/M/G	20.703	173.888

LEGEND:
R=Rookie
Chassis: L=Lola, **R**=Reynard
Engines: F=Ford Cosworth XB, **M**=Menard V6, **B**=Buick
Tires: F=Firestone, **G**=Goodyear

OFFICIAL BOX SCORE • PRIZE LIST • INDY 200

FP	SP	CAR		DRIVER	YR/CH/E/T	LAPS	RUNNING/ REASON OUT	IRL POINTS	TOTAL PRIZES
1	5	12	R	Buzz Calkins	95/R/F/F	200	Running	35	$122,500
2	7	20	R	Tony Stewart	95/L/M/G	200	Running	33	85,250
3	13	54	R	Robbie Buhl	94/R/F/F	198	Running	32	87,250
4	14	33	R	Michele Alboreto	95/L/F/G	198	Running	31	65,000
5	2	21		Roberto Guerrero	94/R/F/G	197	Running	30	59,500
6	12	11		Mike Groff	95/L/F/G	195	Running	29	49,500
7	15	75	R	Johnny O'Connell	95/R/F/F	195	Running	28	46,250
8	11	90		Lyn St. James	94/L/F/G	192	Running	27	48,250
9	16	18		John Paul, Jr.	93/L/F/G	190	Running	26	44,250
10	20	*3		Eddie Cheever	95/L/M/G	184	Accident T1	25	43,250
11	4	41		Scott Sharp	95/L/F/G	184	Accident T1	24	42,000
12	6	14	R	Davey Hamilton	95/L/F/G	173	Accident T2	23	41,000
13	8	17	R	Stan Wattles	94/L/F/F	144	Accident T2	22	40,000
14	3	5		Arie Luyendyk	95/R/F/G	132	Gearbox	21	39,000
15	10	2		Scott Brayton	95/L/M/G	105	Handling	20	38,000
16	9	9		Stephan Gregoire	95/R/F/F	69	Gearbox	19	37,000
17	1	91		Buddy Lazier	95/R/F/F	61	Brakes	18	46,000
18	17	16		Johnny Parsons	93/L/M/F	45	Suspension	17	35,000
19	19	*4	R	Richie Hearn	95/R/F/G	17	Accident T2	16	36,500
20	18	25		Dave Kudrave	93/L/B/G	4	Transmission	15	33,000
		7		Eliseo Salazar	95/L/F/G				10,000
		15		Bill Tempero	92/L/B/G				10,000
		81		Rick DeLorto	92/L/B/				10,000
		26		Jim Buick	92/L/B/G				5,000
		77		Butch Brickell	93/94 L/M/G				5,000

TOTAL: $1,078,500

*Started backup car at end of field after originally qualified car was damaged in final practice.

TIME OF RACE:	1 Hour, 33 Minutes, 30.748 Seconds
AVERAGE SPEED:	128.325 MPH
FASTEST LEADING LAP/ OF RACE:	#12 Calkins, Lap 188: 171.805 MPH
MARGIN OF VICTORY:	.866 Second

LAP LEADERS: #12 Buzz Calkins, 130 laps; 66-70, 76-200; #91 Buddy Lazier, 28 laps; 1-28; #20 Tony Stewart, 27 laps; 29-65; #17 Stan Wattles, 2 laps; 71-72; #14 Davey Hamilton, 2 laps; 74-75; #54 Robbie Buhl, 1 lap; 73.

Legend: FP=Finish Position, SP=Start Position, R=Rookie **Chassis Legend:** L=Lola, R=Reynard
Engine Legend: F=Ford Cosworth XB, B=Buick, M=Menard V6
Tire Legend: F=Firestone, G=Goodyear

STARTING LINEUP DURA-LUBE 200
MARCH 24, 1996

	CAR		DRIVER	CAR NAME	YR/C/E/T	TIME	SPEED
1	*5		Arie Luyendyk	Jonathan Byrd's Cafeteria/Bryant Heating & Cooling Special	95/R/F/F	19.608	183.599
2	4	R	Richie Hearn	Ralph's-Food 4 Less/Della Penna Motorsports	95/R/F/G	19.694	182.797
3	21		Roberto Guerrero	WavePhore, Inc./Pennzoil Reynerd-Ford	94/R/F/G	19.884	181.050
4	20	R	Tony Stewart	Menards/Glidden/Quaker State	95/L/M/F	19.885	181.041
5	2		Scott Brayton	Glidden/Green Tree Special	95/L/M/F	19.963	180.334
6	11		Scott Sharp	Conseco/AJ Foyt Racing	94/L/F/G	19.982	180.162
7	41		Mike Groff	AJ Foyt Enterprises	94/L/F/G	20.441	176.117
8	12	R	Buzz Calkins	Bradley Foodmart/Total Petroleum/MBNA/Logo Athletic	95/R/F/F	20.465	175.910
9	14	R	Davey Hamilton	AJ Foyt Copenhagen Racing Team	95/L/F/G	20.505	175.567
10	75	R	Johnny O'Connell	Ultimate Energy/Distributor of Optima Batteries/MBNA	95/R/F/F	20.611	174.664
11	45	R	Robbie Buhl	Zunne' Group Racing	94/L/F/F	20.773	173.302
12	9		Stephan Gregoire	Hemelgarn Racing	95/R/F/F	20.830	172.828
13	18		John Paul, Jr.	V-Line Lola/Menard	93/L/M/G	20.966	171.707
14	22	R	Michel Jourdain, Jr.	Team Scandia/Canels/Quaker State/Perry Ellis	95/L/F/G	21.038	171.119
15	7	R	Fermin Velez	Team Scandia/Cristal/Copec/Mobil 1/Perry Ellis	95/L/F/G	21.326	168.808
16	96	R	Paul Durant	A.B.F. Motorsports, L.L.C.	92/L/B/G	21.355	168.579
17	16		Johnny Parsons	Linkite/Firestone	93/L/M/F	21.772	165.350
18	27	R	Jim Guthrie	McDonald's/Firestone	93/L/M/F	22.019	163.495
19	64	R	Johnny Unser	Project Indy/Ruger Titanium	94/R/F/G	22.218	162.031
20	15		Dave Kudrave	D.A.R.E.	93/L/B/G	22.363	160.980
21	33	R	Michele Alboreto	Team Scandia/Alta Natural Spring Water/PerryEllis	95/L/F/G	22.408	160.657
22	90		Lyn St. James	Team Scandia/Lifetime/Perry Ellis	95/R/F/G	NT	NS

*New official track record

LEGEND:
Chassis: **L**=Lola, **R**=Reynard
Engines: **F**=Ford Cosworth XB, **M**=Menard V6, **B**=Buick
Tires: **F**=Firestone, **G**=Goodyear

OFFICIAL BOX SCORE • PRIZE LIST • DURALUBE 200

FP	SP	CAR		DRIVER	YR/CH/E/T	LAPS	REASON OUT	POINTS	PRIZES
1	1	5		Arie Luyendyk	95/R/F/F	200	Running	112	$132,000
2	6	11		Scott Sharp	94/L/F/G	*200	Running	114	86,250
3	7	41		Mike Groff	94/L/F/G	*199	Running	122	71,250
4	2	4	R	Richie Hearn	95/R/F/G	198	Running	94	72,500
5	10	75	R	Johnny O'Connell	95/R/F/F	197	Running	116	52,500
6	8	12	R	Buzz Calkins	95/R/F/F	193	Running	128	49,500
7	12	9		Stephan Gregoire	95/R/F/F	190	Running	94	47,750
8	21	33	R	Michele Alboreto	95/L/F/G	187	Running	116	49,250
9	19	64	R	Johnny Unser	94/R/F/G	185	Running	26	44,250
10	20	15		Dave Kudrave	93/L/B/G	168	Fuel	80	45,250
11	4	20	R	Tony Stewart	95/L/M/F	165	Electrical	114	42,000
12	17	16		Johnny Parsons	93/L/M/F	149	Fuel Pump	80	41,000
13	11	45	R	Robbie Buhl	94/L/F/F	148	Header	108	40,000
14	13	18		John Paul, Jr.	93/L/M/G	116	Engine	94	39,000
15	18	27	R	Jim Guthrie	93/L/M/F	115	Accident T3	20	38,000
16	3	21		Roberto Guerrero	94/R/F/G	89	CV Joint	98	37,000
17	9	14	R	Davey Hamilton	95/L/F/G	77	Electrical	82	36,000
18	5	2		Scott Brayton	95/L/M/F	70	Accident T4	74	35,000
19	15	7	R	Fermin Velez	95/L/F/G	32	Contact w/#21 T3	16	34,000
20	14	22	R	Michel Jourdain, Jr.	95/L/F/G	31	Accident T4	15	33,000
21	22	90		Lyn St. James	95/R/F/G	11	Electrical	82	10,000
22	16	96	R	Paul Durant	92/L/B/G	1	Front End	13	10,000
		17	R	Stan Wattles	94/L/F/F			44	10,000
		3		Eddie Cheever	95/L/M/F			50	10,000
		91		Buddy Lazier	95/R/F/F			36	10,000
		36	R	Dan Drinan	92/L/B/G			0	5,000

TOTAL: $1,080,500

*1 lap penalty for entering closed pit

TIME OF RACE:	1 Hour, 42 Minutes, 14 Seconds
AVERAGE SPEED:	117.368 MPH
FASTEST LEADING LAP/ OF RACE:	#5 Luyendyk, Lap 11: 173.152 MPH
MARGIN OF VICTORY:	8.896 Seconds

LAP LEADERS: #5 Arie Luyendyk, 122 laps; 1-24, 75-102, 118-120, 134-200; #11 Scott Sharp, 40 laps; 43-74, 121-128; #45 Robbie Buhl, 20 laps; 103-117, 129-133; #20 Tony Stewart, 11 laps; 25-35; #4 Richie Hearn, 7 laps; 36-42.

Legend: FP=Finish Position, **SP**=Start Position, **R**=Rookie **Chassis Legend: L**=Lola, **R**=Reynard
Engine Legend: F=Ford Cosworth XB, **B**=Buick, **M**=Menard V6
Tire Legend: F=Firestone, **G**=Goodyear

1996 DAILY PRACTICE LAPS

CAR	DRIVER	YR C/E/T	5/06	5/07	5/09	5/10	5/11	5/12	5/13	5/14	5/16	5/17	5/18	5/19	5/23	TOTAL
2	Brayton, Scott	95 L/M/F		50	31	19	23									123
2	Stewart, Tony	95 L/M/F											10			10
3	Cheever, Eddie	95 L/M/F		54	35	12	26							9	6	142
4	Hearn, Richie	95 R/F/G		4	92	41	34					8	23		12	214
5	Luyendyk, Arie	95 R/F/F		56	42		16	18						19	11	162
7	Salazar, Eliseo	95 R/F/G		40	34	28			32					19	15	168
7	Salazar, Eliseo	95 L/F/G			36		25									61
8	Zampedri, Alessandro	95 L/F/G		87	101	22	33		66	50					13	372
9	Gregoire, Stephan	95 R/F/F			68	20	29			23				8	12	160
10	Murphey, Brad	94 R/F/F	124	18	32	18	31	24	25	20		19	20	29	9	369
11	Sharp, Scott	95 L/F/G		31	21	28	31	32		18		12	16		13	202
12	Calkins, Buzz	95 R/F/F	166	26	31	43	25		96			36		52	11	486
14	Hamilton, Davey	95 L/F/G		23	28	33	24			41		21	23		16	209
15	Bell, Justin	92 L/B/G	18		37											55
15	Gosek, Joe	92 L/B/G				19		12	6	10	5	62				114
16	Parsons, Johnny	93 L/M/F			17	18	1						16			52
18	Paul, Jr, John	93 L/M/G		33	54	10	43				46				14	200
20	Stewart, Tony	95 L/M/F	63	7	24	10	24					10				148
21	Guerrero, Roberto	95 R/F/G		20	47	11	26	20	16					9	8	157
21	Guerrero, Roberto	95 R/F/G	16													16
22	Jourdain Jr, Michel	95 L/F/G	113		64	12	34		47	33				10	12	325
23	Brayton, Scott	95 L/M/F										52				52
23	Cheever, Eddie	95 L/M/F							8		67					75
23	Dismore, Mark	95 L/M/F	62													62
23	Stewart, Tony	95 L/M/F								31	70					101
24	Tolsma, Randy	93 L/B/F									25	34	19	30		108
25	Gosek, Joe	92 L/B/G	30		69	13										112
27	Guthrie, Jim	93 L/M/F	108			26	31				11				4	180
30	Dismore, Mark	95 L/M/F	23			38	24							7	8	100
32	Brayton, Scott	95 L/M/F					13									13
32	Ongais, Danny	95 L/M/F													17	17
32	Stewart, Tony	95 L/M/F	39				6						10			55
33	Alboreto, Michele	95 R/F/G	137		47	37	33		33	22	69		11			389

Car	Driver	Spec														Total
34	Salazar, Eliseo	95 L/F/G					6	49	22	49	63		45		234
34	Velez, Fermin	95 L/F/G										34	14	9	57
35	Luyendyk, Arie	95 R/F/F			18				18	62	50	37			238
36	Carlson, Tyce	91 L/B/G	91		80	30	23	21	14	20	25				101
36	Drinan, Dan	91 L/B/G			5		3		17	55		8			187
36	Michner, Andy	91 L/B/G						32			30				102
39	Harrington, Scott	92 L/B/G			39	39	44			38					114
41	Greco, Marco	94 L/F/G	38			15	22			13	22	24		13	225
43	Gosek, Joe	94 L/F/G										26	26	12	64
43	Velez, Fermin	94 L/F/G	15	15				35	65		19		6		134
44	Harrington, Scott	95 R/F/G										88			94
44	Hearn, Richie	95 R/F/G	122		31		15	20	57	75			9		305
45	St James, Lyn	94 L/F/G	15	11		30			51	34	26				223
45	Tolsma, Randy	94 L/F/F	103			22									103
46	Wilson, Rob	93 L/F/G								31	108	51	75		265
52	Matsuda, Hideshi	94 L/F/F										41	22		63
54	Buhl, Robbie	94 L/F/F			80	29	50							18	244
60	Groff, Mike	95 R/F/G	46	46	91	27	29	13	71	59					353
62	Dismore, Mark	93 L/M/F											21		21
62	Ongais, Danny	93 L/M/F											25		25
64	Unser, Johnny	95 R/F/G	50	70	44		24	7			14	53	44	2	354
70	Jones, Davy	95 L/MI/G	29	29	47		40							8	180
72	Jones, Davy	95 L/MI/G			18							42			60
75	O'Connell, Johnny	95 R/F/F					37	67		61	12	73	16	23	289
77	Carlson, Tyce	93 L/M/G											57		57
77	Ongais, Danny	93 L/M/G									30	35			65
84	Boat, Billy	94 L/F/G											14		14
84	Sharp, Scott	94 L/F/G			23				42						23
87	Boat, Billy	92 L/B/G													42
90	Gardner, Racin	94 L/F/G						70						6	76
91	Lazier, Buddy	95 R/F/F	1	40	19	14							9	11	125
93	Gardner, Racin	94 L/F/G	89												89
96	Durant, Paul	92 L/B/G	42	48		11		33						6	175
99	Boat, Billy	94 R/F/G									36	29			165
99	Guerrero, Roberto	94 R/F/G						13		100					13

1996 DAILY BEST SPEEDS

CAR	DRIVER	YR C/E/T	5/06	5/07	5/09	5/10	5/11	5/12	5/13	5/14	5/16	5/17	5/18	5/19	5/23
2	Brayton, Scott	95 L/M/F		235.750	234.070	235.688	232.300								230.621
2	Stewart, Tony	95 L/M/F											233.245	229.399	
3	Cheever, Eddie	95 L/M/F		235.997	234.034	220.442	233.876								223.558
4	Hearn, Richie	95 R/F/G		151.179	231.941	231.440	234.308					229.031	227.946		
5	Luyendyk, Arie	95 R/F/F		233.621	233.143		231.672	237.567						233.633	228.380
7	Salazar, Eliseo	95 L/F/G		228.728	228.438	232.558	232.847		234.858					228.241	230.208
7	Salazar, Eliseo	95 L/F/G			225.236										
8	Zampedri, Alessandro	95 L/F/G		228.932	228.589	225.677	231.137		231.672	230.965					220.864
9	Gregoire, Stephan	95 R/F/F			228.131	222.690	228.397			230.568				227.244	222.392
10	Murphey, Brad	94 R/F/F	209.035	206.555	214.485	221.675	225.231	226.889		228.612	225.875	228.548	226.632	222.343	219.705
11	Sharp, Scott	95 L/F/G		229.539	231.440	235.701	232.132	233.421			225.796	224.349	223.686		227.583
12	Calkins, Buzz	95 R/F/F	227.411	231.839	228.148	234.693	233.973			231.774			226.381	225.507	218.198
14	Hamilton, Davey	95 L/F/G		227.227	226.809	230.864	228.984				219.518	217.712	219.063		211.815
15	Bell, Justin	92 L/B/G	171.389		186.548										
15	Gosek, Joe	92 L/B/G				198.395		202.511	198.522	203.767	123.859	206.219			
16	Parsons, Johnny	93 L/M/F			219.984	223.076	68.968						224.613		
18	Paul, Jr. John	93 L/M/G		224.680	227.038	224.461	227.192				221.511				216.102
20	Stewart, Tony	95 L/M/F	237.336	236.121	237.029	236.004	235.719						232.432		231.273
21	Guerrero, Roberto	95 R/F/G		232.336	229.961	231.428	232.096	229.920	234.308					228.845	214.633
21	Guerrero, Roberto	95 R/F/G		223.076											
22	Jourdain Jr, Michel	95 L/F/G	228.154		229.142	227.141	230.698		234.223	230.610				221.114	218.930
23	Brayton, Scott	95 L/M/F										230.126			
23	Cheever, Eddie	95 L/M/F								218.208	226.489				
23	Dismore, Mark	95 L/M/F	222.283												
23	Stewart, Tony	95 L/M/F							235.837	234.821					
24	Tolsma, Randy	93 L/B/F									186.521	201.113	204.997	214.843	
25	Gosek, Joe	92 L/B/G	189.143		192.897	196.881									
27	Guthrie, Jim	93 L/M/F	209.996			218.055	222.502				172.460				131.631
30	Dismore, Mark	95 L/M/F	228.566			232.702	231.511							226.108	224.411
32	Brayton, Scott	95 L/M/F					233.851								
32	Ongais, Danny	95 L/M/F													226.364
32	Stewart, Tony	95 L/M/F	230.438				234.497						233.245		
33	Alboreto, Michele	95 R/F/G	226.415		227.767	232.186	228.833		230.126	232.192	231.083				219.727
34	Salazar, Eliseo	95 L/F/G					201.010		232.102	228.914	225.626	223.619		227.192	

No.	Driver	Engine	Daily Best Speeds
34	Velez, Fermin	95 L/F/G	203.565, 220.119, 223.392
35	Luyendyk, Arie	95 R/F/F	234.503, 234.870, 234.540, 238.493, 237.774, 239.260, 234.742
36	Carlson, Tyce	91 L/B/G	210.393, 207.737
36	Drinan, Dan	91 L/B/G	209.908, 214.997, 213.159, 212.655, 93.708, 210.694, 215.957, 206.223
36	Michner, Andy	91 L/B/G	206.157, 203.367, 196.631, 190.702
39	Harrington, Scott	92 L/B/G	209.859, 203.804, 192.881
41	Greco, Marco	94 L/F/G	219.106, 218.834, 220.334, 221.549, 227.382, 229.013, 224.512, 225.507, 229.481
43	Gosek, Joe	94 L/F/G	196.421, 223.730, 220.183
43	Velez, Fermin	94 L/F/G	217.802, 223.775, 201.676
44	Harrington, Scott	94 L/F/G	183.001, 225.807
44	Hearn, Richie	95 R/F/G	230.669, 232.378, 233.300, 229.066, 226.592
45	St James, Lyn	94 L/F/G	217.213, 213.336, 226.992, 221.359, 219.245, 225.490, 215.626, 193.357
45	Tolsma, Randy	94 L/F/F	208.923
46	Wilson, Rob	93 L/F/G	214.931, 211.585, 218.755, 192.332
52	Matsuda, Hideshi	94 L/F/F	220.908, 227.192
54	Buhl, Robbie	94 L/F/F	210.931, 216.753, 216.388, 205.630
60	Groff, Mike	95 R/F/G	222.535, 225.045, 230.491, 226.672, 227.049, 229.089, 229.756, 227.434, 227.020
62	Dismore, Mark	93 L/M/F	226.062
62	Ongais, Danny	93 L/M/F	221.904, 200.879
64	Unser, Johnny	95 R/F/G	112.805, 218.235, 219.085, 219.641, 226.535, 227.238, 225.989, 218.627, 224.702
70	Jones, Davy	95 L/MI/G	213.119, 228.798, 234.736, 231.101, 231.696, 224.428
72	Jones, Davy	95 L/MI/G	223.747, 219.405
75	O'Connell, Johnny	95 R/F/F	215.146, 219.850, 222.883, 214.117, 225.315, 219.298, 195.160
77	Carlson, Tyce	93 L/M/G	221.331
77	Ongais, Danny	93 L/M/G	220.194, 208.459
84	Boat, Billy	94 L/F/G	223.786
84	Sharp, Scott	94 L/F/G	227.175
87	Boat, Billy	92 L/B/G	193.690
90	Gardner, Racin	94 L/F/G	209.400, 224.933
91	Lazier, Buddy	95 R/F/F	230.598, 229.926, 233.155, 234.381, 233.161, 230.663, 28.575
93	Gardner, Racin	94 L/F/G	226.165, 223.281, 222.316, 222.420, 213.731
96	Durant, Paul	92 L/B/G	198.347, 211.159, 197.707
99	Boat, Billy	94 R/F/G	224.165, 223.425, 224.657
99	Guerrero, Roberto	94 R/F/G	127.270

1996 QUALIFICATION ATTEMPTS CHRONOLOGICAL SUMMARY

QA	Time	Car	Driver	Lap 1	Lap 2	Lap 3	Lap 4	Four-Lap Average	SR	SP
Saturday May 11, 1996 - Pole Day										
1	2:00	45	Lyn St. James	225.118	224.691	224.781	223.792	224.594		
2	2:05	91	Buddy Lazier	231.493	231.577	231.434	231.368	231.468		
3	2:10	64	Johnny Unser	225.745	225.926	226.455	226.335	226.115	27	*33
4	2:15	8	Alessandro Zampedri	229.592	229.697	229.492	229.598	229.595	2	2
5	2:20	70	Davy Jones	232.943	232.799	232.721	233.064	232.882	19	14
6	2:24	60	Mike Groff	229.089	229.048	228.653	228.027	228.704	24	16
7	2:29	4	Richie Hearn	227.049	226.677	226.364	225.994	226.521		
8	2:34	20	Tony Stewart	233.040	233.179	233.076	233.106	233.100		
9	2:38	18	John Paul Jr.	225.677	219.453	waved off			1	1
10	2:43	12	Buzz Calkins	227.975	228.740	229.662	229.686	229.013		
11	2:51	27	Jim Guthrie	222.305	222.348	222.420	222.502	222.394		
12	2:56	14	Davey Hamilton	228.897	228.804	228.984	228.862	228.887	29	18
13	3:01	3	Eddie Cheever	230.580	231.809	232.210	232.534	231.781	15	11
14	3:06	21	Roberto Guerrero	230.044	232.096	231.660	231.702	231.373	30	19
15	3:09	33	Michele Alboreto	224.143	224.120	waved off			6	18
16	3:14	34	Eliseo Salazar	232.751	232.847	232.498	232.642	232.684		
17	3:19	2	Scott Brayton	231.553	231.238	231.559	231.791	231.535	4	4
18	3:28	22	Michel Jourdain Jr.	228.600	229.873	229.563	229.486	229.380	22	15
19	3:33	9	Stephan Gregoire	226.182	228.125	227.531	228.397	227.556		
20	3:37	30	Mark Dismore	227.032	227.474	227.376	227.158	227.260	16	12
21	4:42	33	Michele Alboreto	228.496	228.091	228.143	228.189	228.229	17	13
22	4:52	18	John Paul Jr.	225.310	224.775	224.809	224.137	224.757		
23	5:27	35	Arie Luyendyk	231.756	233.058	234.742	234.028	233.390	9	7
24	5:42	32	Scott Brayton	233.675	233.536	233.809	233.851	233.718		
			(Car #2 withdrawn prior to run)							
25	5:51	11	Scott Sharp	231.983	232.031	waved off			5	5
Sunday May 12, 1995 - Second Qualifying Day										
26	12:10	5	Arie Luyendyk	227.439	236.239	236.948	237.260	236.986	11	9
27	12:17	41	Marco Greco	228.195	229.218	228.473	229.481	228.840		
28	1:53	10	Brad Murphey	Made a presentation but did not take the green					10	8
29	3:13	11	Scott Sharp	230.533	230.965	231.595	231.714	231.201	14	10
30	3:49	96	Paul Durant	225.034	225.575	226.165	224.848	225.404	3	3
31	4:58	54	Robbie Buhl	226.860	227.049	225.949	225.023	226.217	23	23
32	5:57	90	RacinGardner	224.540	224.933	224.159	224.182	224.453	29	25
Saturday, May 18, 1996 - Third Qualifying Day										
33	11:04	99	Billy Boat	220.604	222.129	222.096	222.475	221.824	36	
34	11:10	34	Fermin Velez	220.897	222.629	223.048	223.392	222.487	32	28
35	11:16	10	Brad Murphey	226.438	224.938	226.210	226.632	226.053	25	26
36	12:11	16	Johnny Parsons	223.353	224.613	224.120	223.292	223.843	30	27
37	5:59	75	Johnny O Connell	222.872	221.724	221.970	222.883	222.361	34	29
Sunday, May 19, 1996 - Bubble Day										
38	4:02	52	Hideshi Matsuda	226.746	227.192	226.740	226.746	226.856	21	30
39	5:37	44	Scott Harrington	222.524	222.949	222.118	221.157	222.185	35	32
40	5:42	43	Joe Gosek	223.730	223.093	222.321	222.036	222.793	31	31
			(Bumps #99 Billy Boat)							
41	5:47	77	Tyce Carlson	218.441	waved off					
42	5:57	77	Tyce Carlson	221.304	220.837	221.331	221.331	221.201	37	

*5/19 Danny Ongais named to drive car qualified by Scott Brayton.

122   QA=Qualification Attempt   X=IRL Car Locked In   SR=Overall Speed Rank   SP=Starting Position

STARTING LINEUP FOR THE 80TH ANNUAL INDIANAPOLIS 500 MILE RACE - MAY 26, 1996

	CAR		DRIVER	CAR NAME	YR/C/E/T	TIME	SPEED
1	20	RY	Tony Stewart	Menards/Glidden/Quaker State Special	95/L/M/F	2:34.440	233.100*
2	70		Davy Jones	Delco Electronics High Tech Team Galles	95/L/MI/G	2:34.585	232.882*
3	7		Eliseo Salazar	Cristal/Copec Mobil	95/L/F/G	2:34.716	232.684
4	3		Eddie Cheever	Quaker State Menards Special	95/L/M/F	2:35.319	231.781
5	91		Buddy Lazier	Hemelgarn Racing-Delta Faucet-Montana	95/R/F/F	2:35.529	231.468
6	21		Roberto Guerrero	WavePhore/Pennzoil Reynard-Ford	95/R/F/G	2:35.593	231.373
7	8		Alessandro Zampedri	Mi-Jack/AGIP/Xcel	95/L/F/G	2:36.798	229.595
8	22	R	Michel Jourdain Jr.	Herdez Quaker State/Viva Mexico!	95/L/F/G	2:36.945	229.380
9	12	R	Buzz Calkins	Bradley Food Marts/Hoosier Lottery	95/R/F/F	2:37.196	229.013
10	14	R	Davey Hamilton	AJ Foyt Copenhagen Racing	95/L/F/G	2:37.283	228.887
11	60		Mike Groff	Valvoline Cummins Craftsman Special	95/R/F/G	2:37.409	228.704
12	33	R	Michele Alboreto	Rio Hotel & Casino/Perry Ellis/Royal Purple	95/R/F/G	2:37.736	228.229
13	9		Stephan Gregoire	Hemelgarn Racing/Delta Faucet/Firestone	95/R/F/F	2:38.203	227.556
14	30	R	Mark Dismore	Quaker State Menards Special	95/L/M/F	2:38.409	227.260
15	4	R	Richie Hearn	Della Penna Motorsports Ralph's Food 4 Less Fuji Film	95/R/F/G	2:38.926	226.521
16	64	R	Johnny Unser	Ruger-Titanium/Project Indy/Reynard	95/R/F/G	2:39.211	226.115
17	18		John Paul, Jr.	V-Line/Earl's Performance Products/Crowne Plaza/Keco	93/L/M/G	2:40.173	224.757
18	45		Lyn St. James	Spirit of San Antonio	94/L/F/F	2:40.289	224.594
19	27	R	Jim Guthrie	Team Blueprint Racing	93/L/M/F	2:41.875	222.394
20	5	W	Arie Luyendyk	Jonathan Byrd's Cafeteria/Bryant Heating & Cooling	95/R/F/F	2:31.908	236.986*
21	11		Scott Sharp	Conseco AJ Foyt Racing	95/L/F/G	2:35.709	231.201
22	41		Marco Greco	AJ Foyt Enterprises	94/L/F/G	2:37.315	228.840
23	54	R	Robbie Buhl	Original Coors/Beck Motorsports	94/L/F/F	2:39.139	226.217
24	96	R	Paul Durant	ABF Motorsports USA/Sunrise Rental Canada	92/L/B/G	2:39.713	225.404
25	90	R	Racin Gardner	Team Scandia/Slick Gardner Enterprises	94/L/F/G	2:40.390	224.453
26	10	R	Brad Murphey	Hemelgarn Racing-Delta Faucet-Firestone	94/R/F/F	2:39.255	226.053
27	16		Johnny Parsons	Team Blueprint Racing	93/L/M/F	2:40.827	223.843
28	34	R	Fermin Velez	Scandia/Xcel/Royal Purple	95/L/F/G	2:41.807	222.487
29	75	R	Johnny O'Connell	Mechanics Laundry/Cunningham Racing/Firestone	95/R/F/F	2:41.899	222.361
30	52		Hideshi Matsuda	Team Taisan/Beck Motorsports	94/L/F/F	2:38.691	226.856
31	43	R	Joe Gosek	Scandia/Fanatics Only/Xcel	94/L/F/G	2:41.585	222.793
32	44	R	Scott Harrington	Gold Eagle/Mechanics Laundry/Harrington/LP	95/R/F/G	2:42.027	222.185
33	32		Danny Ongais	Glidden Menards Special	95/L/M/F	2:34.032	233.718*

* - denotes set new 4-lap track record

33-Car Field Average: 227.807 (1995: 226.912) Faster by .895 mph

LEGEND:
Chassis: **L**=Lola, **R**=Reynard
Engines: **F**=Ford Cosworth XB, **M**=Menard V6, **MI**=Mercedes Ilmor, **B**=Buick
Tires: **F**=Firestone, **G**=Goodyear
W=Winner, **R**=Rookie, **RY**=Rookie of the Year

1996 SCORING POSITIONS AT 10 LAP INTERVALS

Car No.	Driver	SP	10	20	30	40	50	60	70	80	90	100	110	120	130	140	150	160	170	180	190	200	Finish Laps Comp	Running or Reason Out
20	Tony Stewart	1	1	1	1	2	1	4	4	3	21	23	24	24	24	24	24	24	24	24	24	24	82	Engine
70	Davy Jones	2	4	4	4	11	8	7	5	1	7	1	1	1	4	2	2	1	2	2	1	2	200	Running
7	Eliseo Salazar	3	2	2	3	4	2	6	6	6	3	11	11	11	6	6	6	7	7	7	7	6	197	Accident T4
3	Eddie Cheever	4	5	5	5	22	15	19	16	16	19	16	15	15	14	13	12	11	11	11	11	11	189	Running
91	Buddy Lazier	5	6	6	6	1	4	2	2	2	1	2	3	3	3	3	3	2	3	3	3	1	200	Running
21	Roberto Guerrero	6	3	3	2	3	3	1	1	7	5	3	4	2	1	1	1	5	5	1	5	5	198	Accident T4
8	Alessandro Zampedri	7	7	7	8	8	7	5	8	5	4	5	4	4	2	4	4	4	1	1	2	4	199	Accident T4
22	Michel Jourdain, Jr.	8	9	9	9	16	11	11	15	14	12	21	23	21	20	20	19	18	17	13	13	13	177	Running
12	Buzz Calkins	9	16	16	15	15	12	10	14	10	10	7	9	10	7	9	10	15	16	17	17	17	148	Rear Brakes
14	Davey Hamilton	10	11	11	14	7	13	12	11	15	17	22	20	20	19	18	17	17	12	12	12	12	181	Running
60	Mike Groff	11	10	10	10	10	9	9	7	8	6	4	5	5	17	19	20	20	20	20	20	20	122	Fire
33	Michele Alboreto	12	13	13	16	18	29	30	30	30	30	30	30	30	30	30	30	30	30	30	30	30	43	Gear Box
9	Stephan Gregoire	13	12	12	11	9	6	16	27	27	27	27	27	27	27	27	27	27	27	27	27	27	59	Coil Pack Fire
30	Mark Dismore	14	31	28	27	14	17	15	13	13	9	8	7	7	8	17	18	19	19	19	19	19	129	Engine
4	Richie Hearn	15	14	14	13	21	14	13	10	9	13	6	6	6	5	5	5	3	4	5	4	3	200	Running
64	Johnny Unser	16	33	33	33	33	33	33	33	33	33	33	33	33	33	33	33	33	33	33	33	33	0	Transmission
18	John Paul, Jr.	17	32	31	31	31	31	31	31	31	31	31	31	31	31	31	31	31	31	31	31	31	10	Ignition
45	Lyn St. James	18	18	18	22	28	24	23	21	21	20	17	16	16	15	15	14	12	13	14	14	14	153	Accident T1
27	Jim Guthrie	19	25	26	25	20	21	21	20	20	18	15	14	14	13	11	15	16	18	18	18	18	144	Engine
5	Arie Luyendyk	20	8	8	7	5	5	3	3	4	2	12	17	17	16	14	13	13	15	16	16	16	149	Prev. Accident
11	Scott Sharp	21	15	15	12	12	10	8	9	11	8	9	8	8	10	8	7	6	6	6	6	10	194	Accident
41	Marco Greco	22	21	20	23	24	19	20	24	25	26	26	26	26	26	26	26	26	26	26	26	26	64	Engine
54	Robbie Buhl	23	17	17	18	19	18	17	18	18	15	13	12	12	11	10	9	9	8	9	9	9	197	Running
96	Paul Durant	24	28	32	32	32	32	32	32	32	32	32	32	32	32	32	32	32	32	32	32	32	9	Engine
90	Racin Gardner	25	29	30	30	23	26	24	26	22	24	25	25	25	25	25	25	25	25	25	25	25	76	Suspension
10	Brad Murphey	26	26	23	26	26	22	22	17	19	16	18	21	23	23	23	23	23	23	23	23	23	91	Suspension
16	Johnny Parsons	27	23	25	20	6	23	28	28	28	28	28	28	28	28	28	28	28	28	28	28	28	48	Radiator
34	Fermin Velez	28	24	21	21	27	30	26	26	23	23	20	19	19	21	21	21	21	21	21	21	21	107	Engine Fire
75	Johnny O'Connell	29	20	19	17	17	25	27	29	29	29	29	29	29	29	29	29	29	29	29	29	29	46	Fuel Pickup
52	Hideshi Matsuda	30	22	22	19	25	20	18	19	17	14	14	13	13	12	12	11	10	10	10	10	8	197	Running
43	Joe Gosek	31	27	24	24	30	28	26	25	26	25	24	22	22	22	22	22	22	22	22	22	22	106	Radiator
44	Scott Harrington	32	30	27	29	29	27	25	22	24	22	19	18	18	18	16	16	14	14	15	15	15	150	Accident T1
32	Danny Ongais	33	19	29	28	13	16	14	12	12	11	10	10	9	9	7	8	8	9	8	8	7	197	Running

OFFICIAL BOX SCORE • PRIZE LIST • 80TH INDY 500

FP	SP	CAR		DRIVER	YR/CH/E/T	LAPS	TIME	SPEED	RUNNING/ REASON OUT	IRL POINTS	SPEEDWAY PRIZES	TOTAL PRIZES
1	5	91		Buddy Lazier	95/R/F/F	200	3:22:45.753	147.956	Running	159	953,700	$1,367,854
2	2	70		Davy Jones	95/L/MI/G	200	3:22:46.448	147.948	Running	33	468,200	632,503
3	15	4	R	Richie Hearn	95/R/F/G	200	3:22:52.733	147.871	Running	237	322,200	375,203
4	7	8		Alessandro Zampedri	95/L/F/G	199	3:22:09.760	147.653	Accident T4	31	224,800	270,853
5	6	21		Roberto Guerrero	95/R/F/G	198	3:22:10.269	146.905	Accident T4	237	211,800	315,503
6	3	7		Eliseo Salazar	95/L/F/G	197	3:22:11.534	146.148	Accident T4	58	202,100	226,653
7	33	32		Danny Ongais	95/L/M/F	197	3:22:52.255	145.659	Running	28	208,200	228,253
8	30	52		Hideshi Matsuda	94/L/F/F	197	3:22:55.569	145.619	Running	27	209,900	233,953
9	23	54	R	Robbie Buhl	94/L/F/F	197	3:22:55.931	145.615	Running	240	177,600	195,403
10	21	11		Scott Sharp	95/L/F/G	194	3:16:03.946	148.420	Accident	246	183,500	202,053
11	4	3		Eddie Cheever	95/L/M/F	189	3:15:03.728	145.338	Running	147	184,800	206,103
12	10	14	R	Davey Hamilton	95/L/F/G	181	3:22:55.808	133.790	Running	192	166,200	184,003
13	8	22	R	Michel Jourdain, Jr.	95/L/F/G	177	3:22:47.941	130.918	Running	74	162,800	193,653
14	18	45		Lyn St. James	94/L/F/G	153	2:44:40.541	139.365	Accident T1	186	159,300	182,603
15	32	44		Scott Harrington	95/R/F/G	150	2:44:40.641	136.631	Accident T1	20	161,200	190,753
16	20	5	W	Arie Luyendyk	95/R/F/F	149	2:40:17.565	139.432	Prev. Accident	225	178,200	216,503
17	9	12	R	Buzz Calkins	95/R/F/F	148	2:40:22.191	138.430	Rear Brakes	246	150,500	173,553
18	19	27	R	Jim Guthrie	93/L/M/F	144	2:43:51.294	131.824	Engine	74	147,900	168,453
19	14	30	R	Mark Dismore	95/L/M/F	129	2:14:37.437	143.734	Engine	16	160,500	161,253
20	11	60		Mike Groff	95/R/F/G	122	2:09:14.727	141.591	Fire	228	143,200	158,503
21	28	34	R	Fermin Velez	95/L/F/G	107	1:59:33.132	134.251	Engine Fire	60	146,100	176,653
22	31	43	R	Joe Gosek	94/L/F/G	106	2:21:02.003	112.739	Radiator	13	149,100	169,653
23	26	10	R	Brad Murphey	94/R/F/F	91	1:37:15.184	140.355	Suspension	12	162,300	177,853
24	1	20	RY	Tony Stewart	95/L/M/F	82	1:23:05.732	148.022	Engine	204	150,700	222,053
25	25	90	R	Racin Gardner	94/L/F/G	76	1:30:38.258	125.776	Suspension	20	134,300	149,853
26	22	41		Marco Greco	94/L/F/G	64	1:07:18.661	142.622	Engine	9	138,000	153,303
27	13	9		Stephan Gregoire	95/R/F/F	59	1:05:31.343	135.068	Coil Pack Fire	165	131,800	147,103
28	27	16		Johnny Parsons	93/L/M/F	48	54:12.344	132.827	Radiator	141	140,900	161,203
29	29	75	R	Johnny O'Connell	95/R/F/F	47	1:02:41.005	112.470	Fuel Pickup	192	130,000	145,553
30	12	33	R	Michele Alboreto	95/R/F/G	43	47:26.334	135.964	Gear Box	189	129,400	144,953
31	17	18		John Paul, Jr.	93/L/M/G	10	18:29.197	81.140	Ignition	153	128,900	144,203
32	24	96	R	Paul Durant	92/L/B/G	9	9:48.229	137.701	Engine	32	128,600	149,153
33	16	64	R	Johnny Unser	95/R/F/G	0	.000	.000	Transmission	56	128,400	143,953

TOTAL: (1)$6,500,100   (1)$8,114,600

TIME OF RACE:	3 Hours, 22 Minutes, 45.753 Seconds
AVERAGE SPEED:	147.956 MPH
FASTEST LAP OF RACE:	#3 Cheever, Lap 78: 236.103 MPH
FASTEST LEADING LAP:	#20 Stewart, Lap 10: 234.412
MARGIN OF VICTORY:	0.695 Seconds

LAP LEADERS: #21 Roberto Guerrero, 47 laps; 32-37, 55-70, 134-158; #70 Davy Jones, 46 laps; 71-86, 98-120, 159-160, 168-169, 190-192; #20 Tony Stewart, 44 laps; 1-31, 42-54; #91 Buddy Lazier, 43 laps; 38-41, 87-97, 121-133, 161-167, 193-200; #8 Alessandro Zampedri, 20 laps; 170-189.

Legend: FP=Finish Position, **SP**=Start Position, **W**=Former Winner, **R**=Rookie, **RY**=Rookie of the Year **Chassis Legend:** **L**=Lola, **R**=Reynard
Engine Legend: **F**=Ford Cosworth XB, **B**=Buick, **M**=Menard V6, **MI**=Mecedes Ilmor
Tire Legend: **F**=Firestone, **G**=Goodyear
(1) **All-time Records for:** Speedway Total Purse and Total Overall Purse

125

INDY'S CAREER TOP TEN

LAP PRIZE LEADERS

1	Emerson Fittipaldi**	$227,250
2	Mario Andretti*	199,350
3	Michael Andretti	171,900
4	Rick Mears****	144,450
5	Al Unser****	123,200
6	A.J. Foyt, Jr****	97,716
7	Bobby Unser***	82,597
8	Parnelli Jones*	75,050
9	Danny Sullivan*	72,900
10	Gordon Johncock**	67,273

LAP LEADERS

1	Al Unser****	644
2	Ralph DePalma*	612
3	Mario Andretti*	556
4	A.J. Foyt, Jr****	555
5	Wilbur Shaw***	508
6	Emerson Fittipaldi**	505
7	Parnelli Jones*	492
8	Bill Vukovich**	485
9	Bobby Unser***	440
10	Rick Mears****	429

NUMBER OF RACES

1	A.J. Foyt, Jr****	35
2	Mario Andretti*	29
3	Al Unser****	27
4	Johnny Rutherford***	24
5	Gordon Johncock**	24
6	George Snider	22
7	Gary Bettenhausen	21
8	Bobby Unser***	19
9	Lloyd Ruby	18
10	Roger McCluskey	18
11	Tom Sneva*	18

TOTAL MONEY WINNERS

1	Rick Mears****	$4,299,392
2	Al Unser, Jr.**	4,262,690
3	Emerson Fittipaldi**	4,042,767
4	Arie Luyendyk*	3,459,179
5	Al Unser****	3,378,018
6	Bobby Rahal*	2,789,596
7	Mario Andretti*	2,766,931
8	A.J. Foyt, Jr.****	2,637,963
9	Michael Andretti	2,287,921
10	Roberto Guerrero	2,178,763

MILEAGE LEADERS

1	A.J. Foyt, Jr****	12,272.5
2	Al Unser****	10,890
3	Gordon Johncock**	7,895
4	Mario Andretti*	7,625
5	Johnny Rutherford***	6,980
6	Bobby Unser***	6,527.5
7	Cliff Bergere	6,145
8	Lloyd Ruby	6,097.5
9	Mauri Rose***	6,040
10	Rick Mears****	5,855

500 POINT LEADERS

1	Al Unser****	11,000
2	A.J. Foyt, Jr****	10,190
3	Rick Mears****	7,375
4	Gordon Johncock**	6,910
5	Wilbur Shaw***	6,370
6	Bobby Unser***	6,170
7	Ted Horn	6,000
8	Louis Meyer***	5,784
9	Mauri Rose***	5,581
10	Al Unser, Jr.**	5,550

Each * = One Indy 500 Win

PHOTO CREDITS

Altenschulte, Ray Inside front cover,31, 54, 74, 101

Bedwell, Roger 36, 43, 62, 86, 90, 100, 104

Burton, Ron 14, 30

Boyd, Dan 70, 93

Edelstein, Dave 13, 52, 75, 83, 89

Ellis, Steve 14, 22, 27, 46, 100

Haines, Jim 29, 37, 39, 40, 41, 60, 63, 66, 69, 71, 73, 78, 90, 98, 101

Holle, Tim 53, 91

Hunter, Harlen 50, 51, 52

Hunter, Todd 56

Jones, Darryl 6, 33, 34, 36, 40, 43, 45, 47, 49, 52, 53, 63, 65, 67, 68, 70, 71, 72, 74, 78, 79, 81, 82, 83, 85, 86, 87, 88, 91, 93, 94, 95, 97, 99, 105, 127 Inside back cover

Kosofsky, Jamie 62, 77

Kuhn, Walt 6, 9, 10, 11, 12, 19, 28, 34, 46, 47, 48, 53, 56, 61, 82, 102, 103

Lawrence, Jerry 32, 44, 52, 64, 96, 99

Lee, David 48

McManus, Steve 49, 58, 75, 80

McQueeney, Ron 4-5, 6, 8-9, 16, 18-19, 26, 35, 37, 41, 52, 67, 73, 76, 79, 80, 81, 84, 89, 95, 96, 100, 101, 102, 103, 104

Newman, Frank 51

Nichols, Kay 98

Scott, Sam 88, 94

Snoddy, Steve 38, 58-59, 65

Spargur, Leigh 35, 42, 53, 84, 97

Strauser, John 52, 77, 92

Swope, Steve 32, 39, 44, 60, 68, 87, 92, 103

von Burg, Steve 7

Voorhees, Steve 57

Wolfe, Tom 26, 69

Young, Loretta 6

Contributing Photographers: 500 Festival, 50-51

Special thanks to Don Burnstein of The Image Factory for his work on the cover.

Below indicate servicemarks and trademarks of the Indianapolis Motor Speedway Corporation, USA which reserves all rights thereto.

INDIANAPOLIS
500®

LITTLE
500®

GENTLEMEN,
START YOUR
ENGINES®

THE
GREATEST
SPECTACLE
IN
RACING®

INDY 500®

GASOLINE
ALLEY®

INDY REVIEW®

HOME
OF THE
500®

THE INDY®

INDY®

INDYCAR®

INDY LIGHTS®

INDY HEAT®

MINI INDY®

TRADITION

BRICKYARD
400®

**THE
GREATEST
RACE COURSE
IN THE
WORLD®**

**BRICKYARD
CROSSING
CHAMPIONSHIP®**

**BRICKYARD
CROSSING®**

**THE
BRICKYARD®**

**FORMULA
INDY™**

TRACKSIDE™

**LEGENDS OF
INDY®**